SLAYING TAMPA BAY

Curated by Leigh M. Clark

Aurora Corialis Publishing

Pittsburgh, PA

OTHER COLLECTIVES BY LEIGH M. CLARK

Slaying Tampa Bay

Slaying Atlanta

Slaying Nashville

The Dream is in Your Hands

The Dream is in Your Hands: She Can Do It

Living Kindly: Bold Conversations About the Power of Kindness

To all the women who had faith in this project when it was just an idea...

Thank you for being the type of women who support other women and encourage them to follow their dreams. You all deserve to be seen, valued and heard. This book is just the beginning of that mission, and I'm stepping up to make it my priority. I see you, I believe in you, and I will continue to honor you.

With Love and Kindness,

Leigh M. Clark

TABLE OF CONTENTS

Opener 1

    Mandy Schulis 1

What If 7

    Maureen Famiano 7

Rising from the Ashes: Becoming a Nationally Recognized Blogger
and Business Founder 11

    Alyssa Young 11

Finding the Courage to Pursue your Dreams 19

    Kacee Howes 19

Designing a Beautiful Life 27

    Elizabeth Riggs 27

The Mindset for Achieving Your Potential 35

    Jessica Jones 35

Always On Time 43

    Nada Haddad 43

Becoming HER 51

    Ludmila Woodruff 51

Starting Over 61

    Caitlyn Barninger 61

A Passion to Change the World: From Challenging Childhood
Expectations to Global Women's Empowerment 69

    Jennifer Stinson 69

We Attract the Lives We Believe In 79

    Alexandra Valencia 79

We Can't Be Defined 85

    Lora Van Balen 85

Who Knew You Could Improve Your Life without Leaving Your Bed?..93

    Jenna Schwartz 93

The Power of Self Perception... 101

    Bria Patti 101

My Life Reimagined: From Emotional Scars to Empowered Success 107

    Anita Arrendondo 107

Take the Risk..115

    Carrie Williams 115

Life's Echoes Unfiltered... 121

    Dr. Maram Bishawi 121

Trusting & Believing in Me 129

    Parita Patel...129

Onward and Upward.. 135

    Nicole Carver.. 135

New Beginnings 141

    Genesis Krick 141

Closer: Trailblazing Past Fear to Uplevel 149

    Suzanne Duret...149

About the Curator, Leigh M. Clark 157

Opener

Mandy Schulis

Mandy Schulis is a serial entrepreneur with two successful businesses under her belt, an MBA in entrepreneurship and marketing, plus a digital marketing certification. She's a certified, trauma-informed story coach who helps female entrepreneurs bust through mindset barriers and teaches them to leverage their stories for income and impact. Mandy believes in authentic conversation and connection above all else. After launching her third business in 2021, she pivoted from marketing services to coaching, after realizing that many successful female entrepreneurs get stuck in their own stories, often resulting in imposter syndrome and fear of success.

Whether these women are going through divorces, recovering post-partum, or launching a brand-new business, Mandy's superpower is her ability to help them see where they fit into their story. This process embodies Mandy's signature method called The Story Shift. She believes that every story has a purpose and that yours is the key to creating a life full of purpose, profit, and fun. She is a domestic abuse survivor, former single mom, and believer in fairytales. She currently resides in Tampa, Fla., with her husband Matt, kids Ella (12), and Beau (2), and her two rescue fur babies who are always at her feet when she's writing! You can find her at www.mandyschulis.com or under Mandy Schulis on Facebook and Instagram.

———

The thing no one tells you about building a business, about creating YOUR legacy, is that at some point, it will test every bit of your will. Every business owner will be asked, "How bad do you want it?"

It's the question we get when the odds are stacked against us, and we start thinking there's no way we can pull this off. (If you haven't thought this yet, trust me, you will at some point.) There will be a time when you want to say, "Screw this!" and throw in the towel. But you don't. So "How bad do you want it?" becomes the mantra you live by, the phrase that makes you straighten your spine and strengthen your resolve. Because giving up would be worse than never starting at all.

When you have a vision, whatever that might be, failure is always better than giving up.

I know a few things about failing forward. I've treated my journey as an entrepreneur like a case study, a VERY informative experiment. My philosophy is, to quote Thomas Edison, "I have not failed; I have just found 10,000 ways that won't work."[1] The way I see it is that failure isn't really failure, but more like the clarification of a process that I can't see yet. That's the thing about entrepreneurship. It's almost like a sickness. When else would you get excited about falling flat on your face, to only get up covered in figurative mud and confidently proclaim, "OK, that didn't work, but I have an idea!" Then promptly return to the drawing board like a madman, sure that THIS time will be the time that you get it right. And if not that time, then the time after that. It isn't a matter of if you find the way, only when. That surety is something that you only understand if you are following your heart's passion.

It's a damn good thing that the pull you feel—the belief that you are here to serve a purpose—is one that won't be ignored. Otherwise, most of us probably would've given up before we even started. That's not being dramatic, it's just fact. Entrepreneurship is not for the faint of heart, especially when you are in the start-up phase. You become an expert in all kinds of things you wouldn't imagine, from social media to sales pages to searching for grants to help launch your business from start-up to growth.

My guess is that you are hoping to get some amazing stories of women killing it in business, women succeeding, and rising to the top. We will get there, and these stories ARE amazing, but I am going to give you some background and drop some truth on you, too. So, buckle up buttercup... we're gonna have some fun!

First off, my name is Mandy Schulis, and I have the honor of writing the opening for *Slaying Tampa Bay*. I have spent the last few months surrounded by a sisterhood of incredible women whose stories grace the following pages. I'm an intuitive story coach, reiki healer, and mindset mentor. But, more importantly, I

---

[1] A commonly-quoted version of "I have gotten a lot of results! I know several thousand things that won't work," from F. L. Dyer and T. C. Martin *Edison: His Life and Inventions* (1910).

am a woman who has survived and thrived despite it all. We all are. The other trait that many entrepreneurs have—other than what some would argue is insanity—is ingenuity. We create opportunities where others might see a brick wall.

For me, leaving an abusive marriage showed me how truly strong I was. I had already created a successful, six-figure practice as a massage therapist, not once, but twice. I had taken care of my immunocompromised daughter through the entire process. I knew that, come hell or high water, we were going to be OK, even if I had zero idea how that would happen.

There's that idea again... you can see a theme here—this ability to believe in not *if*, but *how*.

I was a massage therapist for over 16 years—and a damn good one, if you ask my clients. But much like my first marriage, I knew I was done with that part of my story long before I admitted it to myself. It's kind of like how you can't un-ring a bell: once a truth is acknowledged and lodges itself in your heart, you can't unknow it. I was stubborn and more than a little mad. The nerve issue that ended my career wasn't just from years of massage. I smiled a little half smile when my clients kept observing that it was unusual that I had the most damage in my left hand, when I was right-handed. While this is true, I know that it wasn't massage that created the issues that left me unable to hold my then-infant son. It was the years of responding to text messages from my ex one-handed, attempting to placate and calm him down.

I've been through enough crap and trauma that we could be here until next year discussing it, but that's not important right now. The important part of going through all this is that I have honed an eerie ability to know when things are coming. Do I ignore it? Of course. Especially when I'm not ready. The universe tends to nudge and then eventually, slap you with the truth. It really doesn't like being ignored. That's what this was for me. I felt like acknowledging it meant that I had to start all over. How wrong I was.

After surgery, I tried doing the "traditional" things that my master's in business trained me for, from social media to copywriting. While I was good, I wasn't great, and I sure wasn't lit up by it the way I had been as a therapist. Slowly, a pattern emerged. So many of the women I worked with (my niche is mainly women) had incredible stories that they vehemently opposed sharing. Especially when that story was the one that would completely catapult their business. An example that still sticks with me is the gut health coach who didn't want to talk about her infertility issues even though they were tied to gut health and ultimately led to her becoming a coach.

It makes things significantly harder for your people to find you if you don't send up "flares" for them; to me, your story *is* that flare.

The intuitive story coach title happened by accident. I'd argue the hardest part of entrepreneurship is explaining what you do clearly, concisely, and with lasting impact. This is especially true for coaching and marketing because there are a million ways to describe it, but you must find the ONE way that resonates best with YOUR people. I swear, you find the way to do that, and the rest is gravy.

That moment happened for me while working with one of my favorite people, a former massage client. She said, "You help me see myself, where I fit into my business. You're like my story fairy godmother." I felt like I got hit by lightning. I knew right then why my massage career was over. It had to be done because I was meant to do something BIGGER. To help other driven women, women that had crazy incredible stories like mine, learn how to tell them. To teach them to send THEIR flares up so business wasn't so damn HARD.

I always tell my clients that if I have told you I'm a domestic violence survivor, a caregiver to my mom, and a former single mom, I have told you a book's worth in just a few words. I have told MY people, HERE I AM... I can HELP. You see, it all comes back to *story*. The stories we tell ourselves, the stories of how we got to where we are... it all matters.

YOUR story matters. What you do with it matters even more.

When I was tapped to write the opening for the amazing women in *Slaying Tampa Bay*, it felt like destiny. After all, storytelling is a big part of what I do, and opening the proverbial floor for these stories is truly an honor. But let's get one thing straight. "Slaying" doesn't mean taking over the world. "Slaying" doesn't mean skyrocketing success. "Slaying" is about cutting a path for the women coming behind you—literally breaking barriers and shattering glass ceilings. "Slaying" is about being willing to send up YOUR flare, to tell YOUR story, and to be the mirror so that those who need to can see you.

"Slaying" isn't about perfection. It's about the hard, dark moments you want to quit. And you refuse to. The moments you don't want to and show the hell up anyway. "Slaying" means you understand that YOU are the hero of your own story. The stories you are about to read are from women who are willing to send up THEIR flare and tell their story so that maybe, just maybe, it'll be what you need to read to keep pushing toward your purpose.

We see you, sis. Keep going.

What If...

Maureen Famiano

Maureen Famiano is an award-winning media specialist, speaker, and author. During her 30-year career that began in New York, she's been a television reporter, producer, and executive producer. In Tampa, she worked at WFLA and WTSP personally booking more than 14,000 guests on her morning shows. Maureen has co-authored several books including a #1 bestselling book on Amazon, *Best Business Minds in Tampa Bay*, and the book *Step Into Your Brilliant Purpose*, which made it to the coveted #1 international bestselling status. In addition, another release, *How to Maximize Your Network*, recently became an Amazon #1 bestseller.

Maureen is a popular speaker at events and has delivered a TEDx Talk on life's journey and the WHAT IF scenario in life and purposeful possibilities. She launched MEFMedia to offer branding strategy, media outreach, and coaching to clients. Her efforts get results. Ellen DeGeneres, *The Today Show*, *Newsweek*, and Lady Gaga's teams have taken notice and featured her clients.

She overcame a huge health challenge in 2010 and 2017 and shares her stage 3 colon cancer journey to inspire others. A 2023 Visionary of the Year Nominee with the Leukemia and Lymphoma Society, she was awarded the Mission Pillar Award for her advocacy and encouraging heartfelt videos about health screenings and being aware of your body and signs. She says her work is not done and she works to encourage others to advocate in their health journey and be the BEST version of themselves and encourages positive outcomes in life with her #TogetherWeWin and #WhatIf mottos.

———

Here's the WHAT IF...

Life is about our journeys. We all have different tentacles of opportunity and possibilities. But it's the decisions we make that lead us down the different paths that define who we are. I like to think that, in life, there are a lot of *what if* moments. There are oh so many wonderful options, that *if* we believe, *if* we give ourselves a chance, *if* we trust in what could be—the discoveries are rich with magical moments of crescendos to reveal exactly who and what we are to be.

My *what if* mantra has been with me all my life, but I didn't always know it. In pausing and looking at how I approached my career, my family dynamic, and my healthcare journey, a theme became clear: I am in control. No one else. I am. If I make decisions or best guesses after careful consideration or guidance, I use my mantra to determine the next step. I also use that vision to help others consider their what if options. We often sell ourselves short.

We might wonder, *WHAT IF I try and I fail? WHAT IF I ask and I get rejected? WHAT* IF it doesn't work out?

I challenge you to instead consider this: *WHAT IF* you ask for a promotion and you get the job? *WHAT IF* you ask a lot of questions during a healthcare journey only to find answers and solutions that you previously assumed were nonexistent? *WHAT IF* those solutions lead to a different outcome?

They just might. They did for me.

Every day we are confronted with options. Do I go here? Do I call them back? Do I take the time to do the task? I challenge you to think of each of those instances or others and reflect on the outcome. What if you did take the time, what if you did do a little extra work, what if you went out of your way to make someone's day?

Where would that lead? Or where *could* it lead?

It's funny, I can really draw lines to instances of meeting someone, attending an event, or sharing kindness and positivity; what happened after these instances was amazing and mind-blowing all wrapped in a big bow. Things happened I wasn't looking for. It's all about *what if*. My own *what if* journeys have led to new rich, warm relationships, to many wonderful invitations, and even to being asked to host amazing events! Plus much more.

In healthcare, my strong will and search for answers led me to find huge solutions many said did not exist. This decision to not give up not only helped me in my own journey, but let me become a voice and reminder to others to embrace their *what ifs*—and believe.

So, as you look at your life, I encourage you to believe in *yourself, your* journey, and to start believing in *your own what ifs...*

You hold the key if you give yourself a chance. My guess is that you'll soar, and be glad you did.

Rising from the Ashes: Becoming a Nationally Recognized Blogger and Business Founder

Alyssa Young

Meet Alyssa Young, a radiant beacon of positivity, the creative mind behind The Unlimited Refills Blog, and the visionary leader behind her business, Katurah Inc. Alyssa is on a mission to empower individuals to replenish their personal well-being with the same dedication they reserve for their morning coffee.

As the founder of The Unlimited Refills Blog, Alyssa's passion for self-care and personal growth shines through her words, inspiring readers nationwide. She draws compelling parallels between the act of refilling a coffee cup and the vital importance of nurturing one's emotional and mental reserves. Through her insightful publications, she encourages her audience to prioritize self-care as an essential need, not a luxury.

Alyssa's innovation extends into the business realm, where she founded Katurah Inc. with the guiding principle of "An Executive Supporting Executives." Her unique approach to leadership and professional development has garnered acclaim, emphasizing the interconnectedness of personal well-being and professional success. Alyssa's holistic vision transcends mere profitability, focusing on elevating individuals to reach their fullest potential.

In a world often consumed by hustle and bustle, Alyssa stands as a steadfast reminder that nurturing one's personal well-being is a journey of profound significance. Her personal journey, catching the curveballs that life has thrown at her, exemplifies resilience, and her unwavering commitment to personal empowerment and professional growth is truly remarkable. Alyssa Young is a force for positivity and personal transformation, leaving her mark and creating an impact in this world.

———

In a world where success stories are often told as smooth ascents to greatness, Alyssa Young's journey stands as a testament to the human spirit's remarkable capacity for resilience and triumph over adversity. Today, she is known as a nationally recognized blogger, the founder of The Unlimited Refills Blog as well as Katurah Inc. where she works alongside executives, a survivor of trauma, a sun-kissed beach resident, and a beacon of hope for women across the nation. But her path to this point was far from easy, marked by trials that tested her mettle, including an aggressive eating disorder, a minor scare with breast cancer, and the constant battle with anxiety.

This is the story of Alyssa Young's rise from the depths of despair to the pinnacle of her dreams.

From a young age, she displayed a natural curiosity and a penchant for expressing herself through the written word. Her parents, recognizing her talent and passion, encouraged her to pursue her dreams and provided unwavering support along the way.

However, Alyssa's path was not without its challenges. As she navigated the tumultuous waters of adolescence and young adulthood, she found herself grappling with an aggressive eating disorder. The illness threatened to consume her, both physically and mentally. But Alyssa possessed a fierce determination to overcome this affliction, and with the support of her family and a team of dedicated healthcare professionals, she embarked on a long and arduous journey to recovery.

Throughout her recovery process, Alyssa discovered the therapeutic power of writing. She began to document her experiences, thoughts, and emotions in a personal journal, using the written word as a means of self-expression and self-healing. It was during this time that she realized the profound impact that sharing her story could have on others who were facing similar struggles. She decided to take a bold step and share her journey of recovery with the world.

Alyssa's decision to open up about her eating disorder was met with a mix of fear and determination. She knew that by sharing her story, she would expose her vulnerabilities to the world, but she also believed that her experiences could serve as a source of inspiration and support for others in need. She started a blog called "The Unlimited Refills Blog," where she discussed the importance of keeping one's personal cup just as full as their coffee cup – a powerful metaphor for self-care and self-love.

In her blog, Alyssa delved into the intricacies of her own journey, from the darkest moments of her eating disorder to the small victories along the way. She offered insights, advice, and a raw, authentic perspective that resonated with readers who were battling similar demons. It didn't take long for her blog to gain traction, and Alyssa's words began to touch the lives of people across the nation.

One pivotal moment in Alyssa's journey came when she received a message from a young woman who had been following her blog. This woman, who had been struggling with her own eating disorder, expressed how Alyssa's words had provided solace and hope during her darkest hours. This heartfelt message reinforced Alyssa's belief in the power of storytelling and the importance of opening up about one's struggles. It was a turning point that solidified her commitment to using her voice to uplift and empower others.

As Alyssa's blog continued to grow in popularity, she found herself at the forefront of a community of women who sought solace and inspiration in her words. She began to receive invitations to speak at events and share her story on various platforms. Alyssa embraced these opportunities, using them as a platform to advocate for mental health awareness, self-care, and the importance of setting healthy boundaries.

One of the most significant challenges Alyssa faced during this period was the constant battle with anxiety. Someone once told her that she would never be successful if she struggled with anxiety. While this remark initially shook her, Alyssa refused to let it define her or deter her from her path. Instead, she saw it as an opportunity to prove that success could coexist with mental health challenges.

Alyssa openly shared her experiences with anxiety on her blog, normalizing the conversation around mental health and inspiring others to seek help when needed. She emphasized that success was not about the absence of obstacles but about the ability to overcome them. Her authenticity and resilience struck a chord with her audience, and her blog continued to thrive.

Despite the hurdles she had already surmounted, life had more tests in store for Alyssa. At the age of 24, during a routine medical examination, a mass was discovered in her breast. The discovery sent shockwaves through her world, and for the first time, Alyssa faced the terrifying possibility of a life-altering diagnosis. It was a situation that demanded unwavering courage and self-advocacy.

Drawing strength from her family, her own resilience, faith, and the lessons learned during her battle with her eating disorder and anxiety, Alyssa confronted the uncertainty ahead. She underwent further medical tests and consultations, determined to face whatever might lie ahead, head-on. The support of her loved ones, the community that she has built around her, and her unshakable determination to continue to rise was the foundation that she stood upon.

A year later, after multiple battles with not feeling well and knowing that something was not okay, Alyssa underwent surgery to remove the mass. The relief she felt upon receiving the news that it was benign was immeasurable. This experience reinforced her commitment to health advocacy, and in sharing her own story, just as she did with her eating disorder.

Throughout her journey, Alyssa carries the memories and spirits of her guardian angels with her. Her Aunt Sherrie, who fought a valiant 12-year battle against stage 4 breast cancer, served as a constant source of inspiration. Her Granny and Papa, who showered her with love, and her Grampy, who always gave her M&M's were cherished memories that fueled her determination to make the most of her life and honor their legacies.

Today, Alyssa Young stands as a symbol of resilience and dedication. She has transformed her personal journey of trauma into triumph, using her experiences to inspire and uplift others. Through her blog, The Unlimited Refills Blog, she continues to spread the message of self-care, self-love, and the importance of setting healthy boundaries.

In addition to her blogging endeavors, Alyssa founded Katurah Inc., a platform dedicated to "An Executive Supporting Executives." Through Katurah Inc., she offers guidance, coaching, and support to individuals in high-pressure executive roles, drawing from her own experiences in managing anxiety and setting boundaries. Her vision is to help others achieve balance and fulfillment in both their personal and professional lives.

In her business, Katurah Inc., Alyssa works hand-in-hand beside a multitude of executives, helping them to navigate the complex world of business, unlock effective strategies, and ensure that their personal and professional lives exist in harmony. She understood that the pressures and demands of executive roles could easily tip the balance, leading to burnout and exhaustion. Drawing from her own journey, Alyssa was uniquely qualified to provide support in achieving that elusive equilibrium.

Alyssa's approach at Katurah Inc. was deeply rooted in empathy and understanding. She recognized that success in the corporate world often comes at a steep cost to one's well-being, and she was determined to change that narrative. She encouraged her clients to prioritize self-care, to set boundaries that protected their mental and emotional health, and to foster a work environment that valued the whole person, not just the professional facade.

One of the key pillars of Katurah Inc. was Alyssa's commitment to helping executives conquer their own battles with anxiety. She firmly believes that mental health challenges should not be obstacles to success but stepping stones to resilience. Through personalized strategy sessions, team-building workshops, and more, Alyssa has empowered her clients to embrace their anxiety, harness its energy, and use it as a driving force toward achievement.

Alyssa's journey with her own anxiety serves as a powerful example for those she works with. She is living proof that anxiety need not be a hindrance but could, in fact, be a catalyst for personal and professional growth. Her clients find solace in her authenticity and her unending dedication to their well-being.

Alyssa also holds a deep passion for mentoring emerging female entrepreneurs, eager to dive into the business realm. Her commitment to nurturing talent reflects her strong belief in the importance of giving back. As someone who's tasted success, she recognizes the value of guiding those newer to the industry, offering insights, and support, as well as sharing her experiences. Alyssa understands that those who have achieved their goals have a responsibility to empower the next generation of female leaders, enabling them to flourish and ultimately strengthen the landscape of women in entrepreneurship.

Alyssa's story is a testament to the indomitable human spirit, to the power of vulnerability and self-expression, and to the transformative potential of sharing one's journey. She serves as a beacon of hope for those facing adversity, reminding them that they too can rise above their challenges and achieve greatness. With every sunset on the beach that she calls home, Alyssa Young continues to inspire and uplift, showing that, indeed, it is possible to turn pain into purpose, fear into strength, and adversity into triumph.

Finding the Courage to Pursue your Dreams

Kacee Howes

Kacee began her career in financial services as an intern with a Fortune 90 company in 2008. Upon receiving a business management and entrepreneurship degree from Clemson University she continued her career with the same company as a financial advisor in the Tampa Bay, Fla., area. Kacee has held many leadership roles at the company and is dedicated to growth. As the district director of the South Tampa office, Kacee focused on empowering her advisors to achieve their personal and professional goals, while serving their clients with world class solutions. Kacee and her team of advisors were recognized as the number two district nationally for the company based on new clients served and policies sold.

Based on her success as a district director, Kacee was appointed as the managing director of the St. Petersburg, Fla., office in July of 2021. Since then, her district office has been recognized as the leading district nationally based on premium and holistic financial planning for the past two years. Kacee is passionate about the Tampa Bay community. She is a Leadership St. Pete alumni, was a co-creator for the firm's diversity and inclusion council and supports efforts in raising money for Alex's Lemonade Stand. Kacee is married to Patrick and has a five-year-old daughter, Isla James.

———

I was still half asleep in the early morning before school when my mother bent down to kiss me goodbye as she left for work wearing a business suit and heels. I'd later come to admire the tenacity and hard work she put in day and night, but as a young girl in a small town, having two driven successful parents was different. It wasn't until I was older and starting my own family that I truly appreciated the sacrifices my parents made and risks they took to provide the best life possible for our family. They were both trailblazers in their respective industries.

After a few years in the classroom, my dad was appointed principal at a low-income and low-performing elementary school. Out of 64 elementary schools in the county, it was ranked dead last when he took over. A former college football player, he was driven not just to be better but to improve his kids' school from the worst to the absolute best. Partnering with city commissioners, the mayor, and local leaders, they painted a vision of what could be, developing a plan to transform the existing school into a premier K-8 charter school of the arts. He turned a failing school into a state-recognized program with a wait list of more than 2,000 students by the time he retired.

My mom worked at the local bank where she was promoted from teller to eventual vice president of business development of a larger bank. After years of dedicated hard work, she eventually decided to leave her stable job and income to further her career. She was the breadwinner of our family but took the risk to start a financial planning practice, with no salary.

I recall our entire family being nervous about the change and how it may impact our lives. However, at our core, we had unwavering faith in my mom's ability to succeed. Our instincts were confirmed, and her new journey wound up being the best decision for our family. What I didn't know then was that her bold career move would lay the foundation for my career path as well.

Shortly after her financial planning career began, I went off to college at Clemson University. During my time there, I struggled to decide on what career path I wanted to pursue. I knew I wanted to have a career that would allow me to make an impact in my community, and I also wanted both personal and financial independence.

I remember having a conversation with my mom, venting about my career aspirations and telling her what was most important in the type of job I was trying to find. She exclaimed, "You are describing my career!" It was at that moment that I realized the opportunity I had been looking for was right in front of my eyes.

I was 21 years old the summer I started as an intern at a Fortune 100 financial planning company. Nervous about my first day on the job, I wanted an outfit that exuded the confidence I feared I couldn't muster. The night before I dashed to the local mall and found a hot pink button up shirt and a pencil skirt. As I opened the daunting doors to that training room, I felt ready. However, staring back at me were 30 other incoming financial advisors, all men, wearing dark suits. I've never felt more out of place, and the looks on their faces seemed as if they were wondering what I was doing there too.

Failing was never an option for me, and I had a fiercely competitive spirit. I knew that if I worked hard, put my head down, and focused on my goals I would somehow be successful. That's what I watched my parents do every day, and it paid off for them. At the end of that internship, I finished as the top producer in my class which eventually secured me a career with the firm when I graduated.

My mom continued in her leadership path as well. She recruited and began mentoring a young advisor, Patrick. He'd left his teaching career to become a financial advisor, and her intuition was telling her we needed to meet. He hesitated, knowing that I was still in school and wondered what might be wrong with me to have my mom push him to connect with me. We wound up meeting later that year at our company headquarters, and what began as a friendship would later turn into our love story. We got married a few years later and started working to build a family. After a year of trying to have a baby, we were thrilled when we finally saw those two pink lines on our pregnancy test.

Excitedly, we told all our family and started dreaming about our future child and the nursery design, as most new parents do. Our nine-week appointment arrived, and things didn't go as planned. Our hearts dropped as we received the news that our baby did not have a strong heartbeat. These are words you are never prepared to hear, but we still had hope.

The next few weeks crawled by like an eternity and at our 11-week appointment we received the news that our baby had no heartbeat. The devastation that day and the days that followed will never leave my memory. So many people in my life had no idea what I was dealing with, but I showed up and hid my heartache.

What should have been a season of excitement and planning turned to grief and anger. I questioned myself endlessly on what I could have done differently.

After two more years of enduring this seemingly endless heartbreak and another second failed pregnancy, I thought it would never happen for us. I threw myself into my work, finding my only peace in outcomes I could control. I built a team and continued to rise in the firm. I was able to create new roles and exceled in my path to leadership. Time flew by, and then I got the news that I was pregnant again.

We were cautiously optimistic this time. It felt like we had waited an eternity, but I had a feeling this time was different. We felt blessed to have this child, and I approached pregnancy this time around with such a different attitude. I welcomed the stretch marks, and my aching feet were a reminder of the blessing I was carrying. The morning sickness was affirmation that my baby was healthy and growing.

Giving birth to our daughter Isla was the best day of our lives. With so much going on as a new mother, I was unaware that my husband had started experiencing unusual pain. He was so focused on caring for me and our new bundle of joy, that he suffered silently.

Our daughter was seven weeks old the day I got a phone call that made my stomach drop. It was Patrick calling from the hospital, and he said I needed to get there as soon as possible. His pain had gotten so intense that he had gone to his physician for the third time in a few weeks when they urged him to rush to the hospital. The endless tests began, and he was admitted that afternoon.

The two of us sat there for what felt like an eternity waiting for someone to tell us what was going on. I will never forget hearing the doctor say he had cancer. My heart stopped and a flood of emotions fell over me, but I held it together for Patrick. We were told he would need to have surgery the next morning followed by four rounds of chemotherapy. Driving home alone that night I wondered how was I ever going to take care of a newborn and a sick husband simultaneously.

The next month of maternity leave was a blur, between doctors' appointments for Isla and Patrick and trying to map out treatment schedules with breastfeeding and going back to work. Part of me was excited to go back into the office just for a distraction and to feel in control again. Watching my husband lay in bed for months, losing his hair and endless pounds off his body weight, I felt completely helpless.

They say motherhood changes you, but motherhood coupled with being a 32-year-old caregiver to a spouse, completely turned my world upside down. Mom guilt was rearing its ugly head at me, and I struggled with knowing what the best thing to do for my family would be. I knew I would feel guilt for working and not being as present as a mother and spouse but also knew I needed to be a rock for our family emotionally and financially since the future was so uncertain.

I knew I had a bigger purpose, and I realized that if I was going to sacrifice even one second away from my family, it had to be because I was doing something meaningful and building something bigger. I had to go all in. I couldn't play it safe any longer, and I needed to raise my hand for a bigger opportunity in the firm. Five months later, I was named the director of our Tampa location, being only one of nine women in the country in this role.

In the years that followed, my husband's cancer went into remission, and our life with our daughter became filled with new happy moments. I believe my hard times and challenges I have faced make me a better leader, partner, and parent today. I know what it feels like to show up and execute no matter how much life may feel like the world is crumbling around you. I've learned to compartmentalize the fear of the uncertain and stay grounded in the moment. It's important to focus on what can be controlled and allow the rest to just unfold.

Today when I kiss my daughter goodbye in a suit and heels, I am filled with pride for the example I am showing her. I've learned on my journey that everything you desire is possible if you have the courage to pursue it.

Designing a Beautiful Life

Elizabeth Riggs

My name is Elizabeth Riggs, and I am the owner of Elizabeth Ashley Interiors located in Tampa, Fla. As a boutique design firm we take on a select amount of projects at a time to allow us to truly understand our clients' design needs and style. We specialize in full-service interior design as well as new construction. With a background in psychology, I want to get into the "design brain" of my clients. This allows me to really add in personalized touches throughout the design. I started Elizabeth Ashley Interiors in 2021. Prior to design, I worked as a rehabilitation and mental health counselor. I worked with adolescents with physical and mental disabilities. As rewarding as it was, it did not feel like my passion. Interior design is absolutely what I am meant to do. I love the joy a beautifully curated room brings to my clients. I am also excited to share that we have recently partnered with the Make-a-Wish Foundation to help them with their room makeovers.

I live in South Tampa with my husband, Matt and our four children. I have two older step-children, Lily (21), and Cole (18). I feel fortunate to have a great relationship with them and feel grateful for the fact that they made me a mommy first. I have loved being their stepmom and watching them grow up. Our two younger boys are Parker (5) and Crew (3). We love to travel and are looking forward to taking the entire family on our first ski trip this coming spring break.

———

Jim Carey once spoke about his belief that as humans we are all creators. We create with every thought, and every word. This has always resonated with me. I believe that we get what we give back. As a parent, I've made it a mission to instill in my children the importance of kindness and doing what's right, understanding that our actions have a ripple effect in the universe.

I'm thankful to have had a childhood that instilled in me a strong moral foundation. We often attended church, and although I didn't realize it as a child, the feeling of community is what was so special and cherished.

My father instilled in me the importance of aligning my priorities in a specific order: first, God; then, family; next, the community; and lastly, myself. This philosophy highlights the value of placing God, family, and community ahead of my personal desires, nurturing a sense of duty, empathy, and a connection to something greater than my individual needs.

Reflecting on these priorities during tough times is a valuable tool for me. It allows me to realign with my core values, ensuring that my actions and decisions remain in line with what truly matters in my life.

Growing up as the youngest of three, and the only girl in the family, I became a curious blend of a tomboy and a lover of all things pink and girly. I cherished moments spent shopping with my mom, just as much as I loved accompanying my dad to the shooting range in the serene countryside. We'd spend entire days running through the woods, and my favorite memories often revolved around grilling hotdogs cooked over a crackling fire.

My mother dedicated herself to our family, and her passion was crafting a beautiful life for us, a truly precious gift. Anything she touched seemed to radiate with beauty due to her remarkable talent. I'm certain that my creativity stems from her. The way she kept our home and made it feel so special would later shape the career I now love so passionately.

Throughout my school years, academics never came as easily for me as it did for other students. I struggled with my focus and test taking. Socially, I did well, and was involved in extracurriculars, but the academics were a challenge. It wasn't until my high school years that I would learn that I had undiagnosed ADD, which made things a bit clearer.

Getting into the University of South Florida was a bit of a challenge. Even though I had a 3.75 GPA and was involved in student council and all sorts of clubs, my college entrance testing would prove to be disheartening. I've never been a good standardized test taker and think schools rely too heavily on them to predict a student's potential.

I was admitted into a six-week summer program at the University of South Florida to assess whether I would be a good candidate for college. As embarrassing as it was to tell my friends this, I was honestly just so thankful to get in. I knew that, as long as I got in, I would put in the hard work and succeed.

I had no idea what I wanted to major in until the first day of my intro to psychology class my freshman year. I was fascinated during the entire lecture. I found that once I started taking more major-related courses, the learning came easier and became more enjoyable. I went on to get my master's in rehabilitation and mental counseling.

I graduated college in 2008 during the biggest global financial crisis since the Great Depression. Finding a job with a bachelor's in psychology was no easy feat, so I decided to pursue my master's degree in rehabilitation and mental health counseling at the University of South Florida. Again, I scored just below the cut-off score for the GRE, but I wrote my acceptance speech about my college experience, and I was accepted! I wrote about how four years of a person's hard work should weigh heavier than one standardized test when determining a person's potential.

During my time in graduate school, I found myself in an unexpected role as an assistant for an investment advisor. It was a career field where I felt remarkably out of place, but it's an experience I'm forever grateful for because it's how I met my husband. I would make special trips to his floor hoping to bump into him at the printer. Little did I know that he came with a seven-year-old son and a nine-year-old daughter who would forever change my life. We dated for two years and in 2014, on the night before Halloween, he proposed to me at the front door of what would become our first family home. We still have a brick from the front porch that we incorporated into our current home's porch

Becoming a stepmom at the age of 26 was never something I had anticipated, but Lily and Cole have been a beautiful blessing since the day I met them.

After receiving my master's degree, I spent seven years working with high school students with physical, mental, and behavioral disabilities. I absolutely loved working with the students and will always cherish that special time. However, there was always a greater yearning to be truly passionate about my profession. I can say that it would take some years, but today I am finally beginning to fully align my passion, my purpose and my profession.

All I ever wanted to be is a mom. After my first son was born in 2017, I knew I wanted to stop working and stay at home with him. I absolutely loved those precious months being home with Parker, but when he was eight months old, I was having lunch with my best friend, Kacee. She was on maternity leave, and we were having wine and talking. I told her that I felt like I was missing something. I felt guilty even saying anything, because all I have ever wanted was to be a mommy.

I loved staying home and not being tied down to a nine-to-five job but also missed having something I was responsible for outside of the home. Kacee asked me, "If you could do anything in the world, what would it be?" As a former counselor working with high school-aged kids, this was a question I asked every single one of my kids but had never really thought about for myself. I answered immediately, "Interior design." She said, "Then DO IT."

But how? I didn't go to school for interior design. How would I even get started? Who would even hire me?

The next week, Kacee sent me a screenshot of a woman we both know who had posted on Facebook that she was looking for an interior designer. That post led to my first design client. Nikki was the first person who took a chance on me, knowing I had zero experience. I will forever be grateful for her blind support.

When she called me two years ago and asked me to help her and her fiancé build their forever home, I was beyond excited. It was such a full-circle moment and one of the best learning experiences. I got my first magazine feature because of her support. Their home was featured in a five-page spread in *The Tampa Magazine*. This was a huge professional accomplishment for me. One of my professional goals has been to have my work published. When asking fellow designers questions about how to get published, I was told it's all about who knows who, so it's best to hire a PR team that knows the right people. I thought to myself, *Why don't I make the right people know me?* So I googled, "Who is the editor of *The Tampa Magazine*," and Leah Ching's name popped up.

I searched for her on Instagram, sent a message to her, simply introducing myself, and sent her a few of the professional shots I had done of Nikki's home. She responded almost immediately! I was shaking as I read her message telling me that she couldn't believe that I reached out because they just had to drop the article they were planning on for next month because of photography issues, and she was about to start sourcing a backup. She told me she loved the pictures and wanted to offer me a five-page spread in the next month's issue!!

I spent the rest of the day crying and thanking God. God said, "Ask and you shall receive."[2] It might not always be on my timing, but God's timing is what matters. I pray that he continues to open

---

[2] Adapted from John 16:24

doors, and I will continue to walk through them with love, light, and support for others.

We recently purchased a lot across the street from our current home that we are planning to build our forever home on. Because we are not planning on building for a couple of years, we thought it would be nice if we tried to plant some flowers, so we purchased five pounds of zinnia seeds and threw them out one evening and prayed they would take off. They did! We now have a beautiful field of flowers for the neighbors to enjoy! We have been told by so many how much they love the flowers. It has been an unexpected blessing that we are happy and proud to share with our community.

Faith, Family, Community, and Design are the cornerstones of my life. Real life experience is the best way to learn any skill and home in your talent. With each new project, I get endless opportunities to grow my knowledge. Learning from mistakes and staying grounded in my convictions have helped me grow my business. What started as a side job for a creative outlet has turned into a full-time business that I am so passionate about and proud of. I prayed that God would bless me with a purpose, and he continues to open doors. I continue to pray for him to use me for good.

The Mindset for Achieving Your Potential

Jessica Jones

Jessica is a female entrepreneur based in Tampa, Fla. As a passionate intimate portraiture photographer, she specializes in a photography experience that accentuates self-love and radical self-acceptance through a feminine fine art experience. She is a soul-searcher who strives to make genuine connections with others and nurture relationships with family, friends, and the community. As a true testament to her business vision of empowering and celebrating women, she actively participates in community charities that support the well-being of women.

Jessica is a firm believer that the scope of our happiness is based upon our mindset and perspectives. She is proud of life's challenges and her ability to navigate them with grace and tenacity. She is a boasting mother to a seven-year-old boy who is the source of her smile. When she became a mother, she felt her life shift in a way that enabled her to feel a deeper capacity for love and motivation for the fulfillment of life's potential.

When she isn't in her studio, she enjoys watching her son grow, spending time with friends, and traveling. She is a proud resident of ever-flourishing Tampa Bay where she was born. As an eager-to-grow entrepreneur, she enjoys fostering relationships with like-minded people who also view life as big and complex rather than small and simple. She believes the more we grow and accomplish, the more we can make a positive impact on the world around us. She strongly encourages everyone to have a mentor and to become a mentor.

———

If you love what you do, you'll never work a day in your life "without purpose." I spoke about being a photographer for years before becoming a photographer. I had a stereotypical picture-perfect life on the outside: the house, cars, husband in a suit, and an adorable baby who everyone complimented.

This was life for me at 25.

I would rarely share this insight with others and now I am publishing my vulnerable story for the public to read. I do not like victim labels; I do not define myself by what went wrong (if so, it would surpass the 1,500-word limit). The foundation of my earlier business is the downfall of this one. It wasn't easy, but it was my core values and the adversity I faced that made me the woman (and business owner I am today).

When I became a single mother (and primary custodial parent) in this world of abundant stress and responsibility, I was more motivated than ever to be the best version of myself. I can't count the number of times people have judged me for choosing a challenge; it's true what Maslow says, only about two percent of society strives to achieve their full potential. A lot of people will choose complacency, dysfunction, and the path of least resistance.

I believe most of us fall into one of two career streams: we choose to be entrepreneurs or choose to work for one. Either can create a good life.

I started my endeavor in entrepreneurship because nobody cares what your circumstance is, and nobody will help you more than you can help yourself. I wanted to be present in my child's life, while also laying the foundation for his future (and so often a parent's occupation requires them to choose one or the other.) I frequently get asked how I got into the boudoir photography industry—it is intriguing to people that I spend a lot of my time with clients who are partially unclothed. I love this question, and always appreciate the opportunity to express my passion.

I tried a lot of different genres of photography, which is normal; many aspiring artists do not initially have a defined direction. I found that with boudoir shoots, I was in my element; it was a flame that grew brighter, and this was a direct result of the expression of my client's experiences. Before clients even step foot into my studio, I get continuous opportunities to meet women on a vulnerable and authentic level (this is rare, as so many of us are guarded). They choose to hold an unwavering trust in me as a person to whom they disclose their "why" for their intimate artistic portraiture experience. They also choose to invest in me professionally.

On the day of my client's photography session, they spend about four hours with me, ultimately resulting in an image reveal of the portraiture session. This is one of the parts of this business that defines who is meant to be working in this type of position: as photographers, we are given the opportunity to experience real and vulnerable emotions from clients. To be successful, we must have the capacity to hold this space. I have seen hundreds of women smile, cry, and celebrate to different degrees when shown a glamorous and raw image of themselves. I have consulted numerous clients in their intentions to create intimate imagery as a milestone gift for a partner or the journey to strengthen a marriage through creating imagery for their spouse. What began as a shot in the dark of a photography journey ended up as the universe guiding me to a medium of art that has given me the opportunity to make an impact, and genuinely fulfill a purpose.

As I said before, I believe that you either become an entrepreneur or you work for one. I chose to become one as a direct reflection of my own prerogative. I have always been called an old soul: I enjoy viewing life as big and complex rather than small and simple. Entrepreneurship requires so much of you and ultimately offers the ability to grow. As an entrepreneur, you must be adaptable, accountable, stealthy, eager, and more.

But without the opportunity to analyze myself and set and accomplish goals, I do not feel like I am striving to be in Maslow's state of self-actualization (with the two percent of us he said ever get there). I think each person deserves recognition for where they are in their journey; if you didn't choose the path of entrepreneurship, you're still relevant, worthy, and able to soar to new heights. My own passion for entrepreneurship is relevant to my personal path and complexities; it was the solution to my problem and created an opportunity for optimal growth.

If you've ever been prompted to answer the question, "What is something you would tell your younger self?" Or, "What is something you would tell someone who is ten years younger than you?" My answer would be that mentorship is important. I believe that the best thing you can do to achieve growth in any occupation and to grow in all directions of life is to find excellent mentors. Someone always has the answers to your questions. Someone can always reflect upon being at your phase of development occupationally or interpersonally, and they have the ability and willingness to guide you.

You must use discernment when choosing a mentor: be sure to choose someone you trust and believe wants to see you achieve your full potential. The next step is to become a mentor yourself.

Mentorship is not about providing unsolicited advice or assigning yourself to be someone's unlicensed therapist (that is codependency). I am thankful to have the mindset of inspiration (rather than envy) because I am inspired by women wherever they are in their journey. I find great joy in building authentic connections and gaining insights from accomplished women who, more often than not, share commonalities: they overcame challenges and hardship, they have a growth mindset, and they made something spectacular grow into fruition.

When working alongside my boudoir clients I use my artistry and interpersonal skills professionally as well as in a mentorship role. I guide the clients through our studio process as well as achieve the goal of many artists and turn my photographs into a physical piece of artwork, the tangible products that our clients receive. Having the opportunity to serve many clients, we now have a solid reputation for credible artwork that is worthy of being on someone's coffee table, displayed on their walls, and even given as gifts on one of their most beloved celebrations: their wedding day.

When I dove face-first into the world of boudoir photography and became a full-time artist, I had no clue the amount of mentorship that was waiting for me. I needed to be able to educate myself on having a functional business and just like many other industries, this one had a community of entrepreneurs that were teaching and guiding each other. If you know someone who owns one business, they likely have other business too (or will). Entrepreneurial humans are ever-evolving, just as the world around us is. We don't grow when we always sit at the same table, so now I am entering new rooms and networking with women in various industries. When I network with women, I do not see them as clients or transactions, I see them as a whole world within another person, and I am thankful if they give me the opportunity to learn their story.

One superpower I am still wrapping my head around (because it is so powerful it doesn't seem real) is the law of attraction. We have so much power and magnetism in our minds and our hearts. In the words of Paul Coelho, author of *The Alchemist*, "When you want something, all the universe conspires to help you achieve it." Another relevant quote from *The Alchemist*: "Before a dream is realized, the soul of the World tests everything that was learned along the way. It does this not because it is evil, but so we can, in addition to realizing our dreams, master the lessons we've learned as we've moved toward that dream, that's the point at which most people give up."[3]

I want to reference the above mention of Maslow's theory on the two percent, when most people are challenged and tested, they do give up. But with a mindset to grow, you will view these experiences as pertinent lessons, the building blocks to achieving your potential.

When assigned a deadline for this essay that you are reading, I had months to write this. I want to confess that I wrote this entirely a day before it was due and not because I strive for

---

[3] Coehlo, Paolo. *The Alchemist*. HarperOne Publishing, 1988.

procrastination. I was excited to be a part of this project, but I was waiting for a serene "right time" where there would be no interference and an empty itinerary; that never happened. If I set all my goals for taking action only in moments of serenity and perfect circumstances, they would never happen.

Many people deny themselves the opportunity to grow and become their best selves because they are waiting for the right time. But the few who see the opportunity to grow, become, and accomplish through all of life's lessons have the reward of making the best of this life.

Always On Time

Nada Haddad

Nada S. Haddad is an attorney, a naturally gifted public speaker, and an entrepreneur. She introduces herself as, "Nada, Not Nothing," due to the common misapprehension of her name. Nada has worked professionally as an attorney across the United States and spent several years working in government. Prior to obtaining her law license, she spent many years working in various industries creating a broad background in business development, marketing, branding, and the legal industry. She has mastered the art of networking and building and maintaining relationships through her travels around the globe. Nada has spent most of her life coaching and building up others. She is a fierce advocate for the voiceless and is dedicated to transforming the lives of those around her and in her community. It is her hope to leave the world better than how she found it. Nada believes, "God created us all to mean something, not nothing. As such, it is our job to be the beacon of hope and compassion to all, particularly to those most vulnerable."

Nada was born and raised in Tampa, Fla. She graduated from The University of Tampa with her bachelor's degree and went on to obtain a juris doctorate from Florida Coastal School of Law. She is also a licensed real estate agent, a licensed notary, and sits on the board of six different organizations and nonprofits throughout Florida. She is a linguaphile and speaks several different languages. Nada has a large, loud, and loving family with Lebanese roots. Most family gatherings are centered on the kitchen and a shared meal. She loves to cook and entertain for her family and friends, and spends her free time traveling, in the outdoors, or with her side-pup, Coco the Yorkie.

Although her path has been less than traditional, Nada firmly abides by her mantra, "You are always on time."

———

Not many of us like to talk about what it feels like to be "stuck" or what it feels like to be at a point of transition in your life. In fact, most people avoid doing so. Today, we live in a world of social media highlight reels and living a curated "success sells" lifestyle filled with influencers and filters. This story is meant to give an unfiltered glimpse into what is normally a filtered world.

My name is Nada (pronounced like "Neda"). I spent most of my life hearing, "'Nada,' like 'nothing'?" I still cringe when I hear someone ask me that, partly because, if you hear something enough, you begin to believe it. For 30-something years, I believed I was nothing.

I grew up in a large, loud, and loving Lebanese family, in South Tampa, a small and affluent town on the Gulf Coast of Florida. In 1980, my parents immigrated to the United States from Lebanon amidst a civil war in pursuit of a better life.

In my formative years, I was a shy, quiet, and sensitive bookworm. As I grew older, I became involved in sports and extracurricular activities. I was an honor student with a large social circle. But what many of my peers did not realize is that my life behind the scenes was very different. I grew up in a conservative Catholic household with a very strict set of rules. However, I dealt with more than my fair share of obstacles. I've lost friends to addiction; I learned about death and grief at a very young age; I've struggled with my body image and self-confidence; I started working at the age of 12; I wore hand-me-downs and didn't always fit in; I struggled a lot with my faith; and unfortunately, in my college years, I was a victim of sexual assault.

In my mid-twenties, I experienced a "quarter life crisis" and moved to Southeast China with some friends I met in college. Little did I know, it took moving across the world to learn I had the ability to be brave. Eventually, in my early thirties, I achieved my dream of becoming the first attorney in my family. In late 2018, I accepted a job offer in Texas. I never thought two days later, I would be rushing my father to the emergency room. He suffered a massive heart attack, and had I not been there, he would have died. I was right on time.

My dad pushed me to move as planned. I had to be brave. So, I packed up everything in my black and maroon Toyota FJ Cruiser, and off I went. While practicing immigration law, I applied to the Peace Corps, and after a few short months, I lost my job. Again, I had to be brave. I accepted a job in California, where I represented mostly deaf clients around the country, seeking asylum. In late 2019, I made my way back to Tampa, and just before my departure for the Peace Corps, COVID happened. I felt like one more opportunity was taken away. I was broken, again.

At the time, I thought I knew what I wanted. But looking back, God knew where He wanted me to be. In the fall of 2021, my father, my best friend, died tragically and unexpectedly due to complications from a surgery. My world ended, but the world I lived in kept going. I had to be brave, not just for myself, but for my widowed and loving mother.

When I was approached to be part of this book in the early summer of 2023, I felt like a complete imposter, totally unworthy. Who would want to hear my story? Who am I to write a book? Where am I in my life to think that I have achieved success to be a role model for other women? I had nothing to show (at least it felt that way). I was in my mid-thirties, struggling financially, I had no job, no business or prospects, I was living at home, single and overweight. At the time, it seemed like nothing but shame coursed through my veins.

The weight of the world was on my shoulders, and it was crippling my ability to function. I did not think it could get any worse. Then it happened: In a two-week span, a series of events occurred that tested my faith.

I lost my only aunt six days after the two-year anniversary of my father's death. A few days later, a driver ran a red light and totaled my FJ Cruiser. And in the middle of my aunt's funeral, my brother-in-law unexpectedly lost his mother.

I felt depleted and overwhelmed. But totaling my truck shook me to my core. To be clear, it wasn't the loss of my truck that shook me, but what she symbolized. I referred to my truck as a "she" because she was strong, reliable, dependable. She was everything I needed her to be, and everything I wanted to be. I can still hear the explosive crash of my truck against the other driver's vehicle. My front end crumpled like an accordion, spilling fluid the color of blood onto the road. The eerie part was that the spilled fluid was in the shape of a heart, as if she was stabbed, as if I were stabbed.

She was with me through everything I overcame over the past ten years. She drove me to safety when I escaped an abusive relationship. She moved me to law school, across the country, and up and down the east and west coast of America. Together, we saw every inch of Florida. I chauffeured family, friends, and even strangers who needed a lift. I drove my nephews, my friends, and their kids in it-blasting songs and singing so loud people would stop and stare. I drove her in silence, with the windows down and no destination, when I needed a break from taking care of my dad in the trauma intensive care unit during COVID. We took countless adventures with my side-pup, Coco hanging out the window with her hair blowing and tongue dangling. She heard me scream and curse until I was hoarse; she saw my tears fall like rain, until they ran dry. I slept in her when I needed shelter, and she helped me feel safe when I had to change (literally and figuratively).

For ten years, my truck was the only consistent thing I had; she was my protection and the only asset I owned. She was mine. Losing her felt like I had absolutely nothing left. I felt trapped. I had no safe haven to escape to and whisk me away when I wanted.

Many of us may struggle with questions and guilt like, "How could I allow myself to feel so defeated and depressed when there is so much to be thankful for?" People would say, I have so much to offer, but why didn't I see that? I am this amazing, intelligent, beautiful person who is loved by so many, but I did not see it for myself. The thing is, none of that matters when you don't truly see who you are. You just sit there, in a puddle of tears, broken, lost, and afraid, barely treading water. You do just enough for people to think you are living your best life. Yes, I have letters behind my name. Yes, I have other certificates and accomplishments. But we are all human and have seasons of defeat.

My accident changed me. I made a decision and a promise to myself: I would no longer be a victim, but a victor. I may not know what is next, or where I am going, or what I am supposed to do. But what I do know is that my worth is not defined by society, my circumstances, social norms, the job that I have, the car that I drive, and certainly not the opinions of others. I decide what I am worth because my brain only believes what I tell it to. I am fearfully and wonderfully made by my Creator.

I shifted my priorities by putting myself first, loving all of who I am, past, present, and future. Those traumatic events that I thought broke me, only rebuilt me. I chose to immerse myself in my community and a strong network of faithful friends, deepening my relationship with Christ. I decided to harness my energy in utilizing my connections to make a bigger impact and transform my community in various Christian-based organizations. I have also realized that the conventional route is not always the ideal route; it's not about the destination, it is about the journey.

Please believe that there is no shame in where you are today. Someone once said, "There is beauty in the brokenness." Whether you're broke, broken, or battered, when those pieces are put back together, they may not be perfect. But life isn't about being perfect, it is about being perfectly imperfect. It is about making yourself whole again, broken pieces and all.

I am so grateful to God for the opportunity to spend this precious time with my mom as roommates. These are the moments we must cherish and hold onto. I am blessed beyond measure for my incredibly loving and supportive family and friends who have surrounded me and built me up. I am equally appreciative for my "earth angels" who have crossed my path when I didn't know I needed them. I only hope that I have been able to give to my friends and family as much as I have received from them.

I pray a lot, I pray hard, and I ask God to show me His way. Sometimes God does not give us what we think we want, but He gives us what we need. I may not know exactly what the next chapter holds, but for now, this is exactly where I am supposed to be.

I will leave you with a couple Nada-isms that keep me going and I hope will do the same for you:

You must believe that YOU are something, not nothing! You have an incredible gift to share with the world, don't hide it. I want you to recognize your "something" and share that with those who feel like "nothing."

Your story matters. When you choose to be open and transparent, you can literally change someone's life. How great of a gift is that?

It is ok to not be ok. Read it again.

There are no accidents or coincidences in life, just divine timing.

There is no shame in asking for help. Even if it feels like you have no one, I promise that earth angels will show up.

Lastly, regardless of who you think you should be, or where you are supposed to be in life: you are never late, you are never behind, you are right where you are supposed to be. YOU ARE ALWAYS ON TIME. Believe every single word.

From the bottom of my heart, thank you for giving me the space to share with you a small part of my journey. This book would not exist if it weren't for you. I am eternally grateful to you, whoever you are, wherever you are.

Becoming HER

Ludmila Woodruff

Ludmila Woodruff is a relationship and intimacy coach who coaches high achieving women who want to be as successful in their relationships as they are in their careers or businesses. She offers trauma informed and radical self-responsibility coaching because she believes that relationships define the quality of your life and every single one of them starts with you.

Does it seem you have it all, but you find yourself feeling frustrated, emotional, anxious, and overwhelmed with yourself, your partner, your kids, your parents, or your dating life?

Ludmila knows you are the solution to the emotional pain and disconnection you are experiencing. She works with high-achieving women who feel like they are stuck, who want more out of their lives and relationships and desire support in finding a way to move forward without fixing, pleasing, overdoing, or controlling people or situations.

Her coaching approach is holistic. She will work with your mindset, your nervous system, your sensuality, sexuality, feminine and masculine energy, and your inner child so you can feel fulfilled, calm, magnetic, connected, supported and loved.

———

You are and have always been *the one.*

I remember attending high school in Poland and sitting at my desk, wondering what my life would become. I wondered who I would be after high school, all the places I would go, and even the home I would one day be able to call my own.

Growing up, I never seemed to fit in.

I was born in Poland to a Russian mom and a Polish father during a time when people hated Russians. Russians tended to have a bad reputation for being cold, but it never bothered me. Although I never seemed to quite fit in, I got along very well with others, much like I do today.

As far back as I can remember, I have been fascinated with people and intrigued by human behavior. I would often sit and ponder why people do the things they do, how we all interact with one another, and the way we engage and build relationships.

My parents gave me a Russian name, my grandmother's name. Ludmila means "love of the people." Love is what I aspire to embody in my being and in my work.

I have always been a dreamer. As a young girl, I loved reading and watching romantic stories. I remember wishing a knight on a white horse would save me and we would ride off into the sunset together. I wasn't sure when he would arrive, or where he would come from, but it was a beautiful fantasy that was so far from my reality at that time.

Just a few years later, after graduating, I stepped off a 24-hour bus ride in Antwerp, Belgium. As I made my way off the bus, a breeze made me consciously aware that I was far from home. The uncertainty of what was ahead of me triggered fear—but simultaneously enticed me with an excitement that made me shiver. At 19, I arrived in a new country, where there was a brand-new culture and a foreign language. I was alone and I didn't know a single person.

This is where the young girl within me became a woman. I didn't understand yet, but the moment I stepped onto Belgian soil, I was *the one* to start the journey of *unbecoming* in order to authentically *become* who I was destined to be.

I had embarked on a single-soldier journey of unlearning, healing, grieving, growing, and

evolving. Being in a brand-new environment gave me the emotional, mental, and spiritual capacity to process pain that I had pushed aside before.

I recalled coming home to our family's small apartment in Wroclaw, Poland. I was returning home from the nearby playground when I saw my mom and grandma; they were completely pale. Abruptly and without much emotion, my mother said, "Your sister is dead; we just received a phone call from Russia."

I stood there frozen, not sure how to take the news. I went outside again, where a friend was waiting for me. I sat next to her on the staircase and said "I don't understand but my sister is dead." I was nine years old.

I was *the one* to start healing this sister wound so many years later.

I recalled another moment when my dad held me for the last time when I was three years old. I don't remember him much, but I know that he is always with me. He is there when I make decisions that stretch me and make me feel uncomfortable, but compel me to evolve into an elevated version of myself. When I look at our pictures together, I fall into a deep sense of belonging, and I'm reminded of being held in his arms. This is still my love language.

Both my father and my sister died in car accidents. This memory affirms to me that I was *the one* to start healing the masculine within me, and that I didn't need to live my life on guard, constantly fearing the loss of love.

I knew that I had finally overcome this fear one evening while sitting in a bar in Antwerp with four Polish friends. We were laughing as always, celebrating our wins and our challenges. We always had to sit in the back because our charisma and energy were so electrifying everywhere we went. (Belgium is a country where people appreciate the calm and more introverted ways of being—my friends and I were explosive balls of abundant energy!)

My amazing friend Basia mentioned her friend Douglas who, according to her, was a phenomenal man. In that split second, I felt my body remember him: we had met a year earlier during a time when neither of us was ready for the relationship we have today.

As Basia and I talked, I realized I was open and ready for the right man to come into my life: I had done the internal work, was crystal clear on my values and non-negotiables, clear about my worth and what I deserved. When I healed my heart, it became a gift to the man who was whole within himself and had the capacity to love me properly. Now we joke that I reached out to him on Facebook Messenger—but he is the one who replied and kept following up and organizing the dates. He won me and my heart over. The rest is history.

Thirteen years, 12 married years, two kids, and four moves later, we are stronger than ever before. I wish this for all the high-achieving women out there. You *can* have it all. The love, the career, the financial stability, and the family you dream of.

Today I help clients heal their father and mother wounds. The loss or lack of one parent (or both) is imprinted in the bodies, hearts, and subconscious minds of those who have suffered neglect, abandonment, and/or abuse. Our parents are supposed to nurture, love, and protect us, and when this does not happen, we must do the work to heal. Moving towards forgiveness, integrating grief into unconditional love, and creating a relationship with the divine feminine and masculine is a gift that I help clients find for themselves.

I know what it's like to long for a place where you really belong and to crave deep connection with those around you. I also know the power of learning to love yourself deeply, which allows true love to radiate from the inside out.

In June 2011, I cried tears of joy and felt an overwhelming sense of love and abundance when I held my firstborn son for the first time. No words can truly articulate who I became in that exact moment. No book, podcast, or TEDx talk could have prepared me for the heart expansion that you experience when you are skin-to-skin and heart-to-heart with a little human you know you will love for the rest of your life.

Nothing could have prepared me for the sanctuary of motherhood. When you become a mother, you are hardly ever the same. You continue to evolve. I was a different person when we welcomed our second son in 2016. I was a different woman inside and out.

My journey of returning home to myself, attracting love, and understanding the power of nurturing deeply connected relationships started at a very young age. Losing a parent leaves a deep longing for love and connection in the absence of the lost loved one. Sometimes I would feel glimpses of grief as a result of this unmet longing. When I would be at the zoo and see families walk with both parents laughing, or when visiting my friends who had this blessing as well, I would be reminded of the fact that I did not have a dad, and would miss him deeply during those moments.

The desire to heal my heart around men and masculine energy got very loud at the end of my last relationship, just before I met my husband.

I was *the one* to rewrite the generational story of marriage and relationships.

What was supposed to be a one-year experience in Belgium turned into 15 years of living and learning Dutch and English fluently, making friends from all over the world, understanding the world from a much wider perspective, and blending my Polish and Russian roots with international flavor.

Taking the leap and daring to do life differently, I left home and pursued the beautiful life that I used to fantasize about as a young girl. Instead of waiting on a knight in shining armor to ride up and rescue me, I decided to save myself. Early on, I knew there was more to life for me, even though I wasn't completely sure what it would look like. I was the one taking the big leap without any "proof" that more would be available for me; I just believed that there could be a better life ahead of me than what was behind me and was bold enough to go after it. Today, I am typing my story that I get to share with you from my gorgeous home that I have been able to create with my husband. My home in Tampa is filled with deep connection and the warmth of our two sons.

I was *the one* to rewrite the understanding of what was possible—and because I believed in and took inspired action towards the life I dreamed of, I get to embody it today. I finally

found my knight—well, he found me, but I saved myself first.

When you save yourself, you rescue your dreams, and reclaim your destiny. My soul knew that starting a life and relationship coaching business would be a challenge as I have never run a business and have never been around entrepreneurs. I remember expressing my desire to launch my business and being met with the question, "Who is going to pay you for that?" It felt like a punch in my stomach.

Two years later I helped that same woman and her husband prevent a divorce and restore their marriage so their kids could have a beautiful family and be raised in an environment where the legacy of love and relationships were modeled. I was *the one* to first heal my own wounds and then help others change their relationship, love, and family trajectory.

My business has been born from a deep desire for myself and my own family to be the best we can be. Even though I felt a lot of darkness, I always kept looking for solutions, and a deeper understanding of my feelings. Doing this is how I discovered my pathway into coaching. I felt an innate eagerness to feel fulfilled, joyful, deeply connected, and sensual. So I mastered the art of feminine communication, and it brought me *home* within myself even more.

Love, relationships, deep connections, and creating a better world one person, relationship, family, and community at a time has always been a leading thread of my being and soul mission.

My destiny has always been to become exactly who I am today with an urge to continue becoming; it's been a culmination of being a mentor, a coach, and a healer. I believe that the impact of following my calling will last for generations.

I show women how to be sensual goddesses. I open them up to the feminine and help them feel sexually satisfied and deeply connected. I want them to become high-vibrating queens in all relationships, while making an incredible impact in the world and being financially abundant. This is my gift to the women I serve, and my personal lifelong commitment.

My mission in life is to support as many women, relationships, and families in healing their hearts and minds. I want them to have thriving, breathtaking connections, regulated nervous systems, flourishing communication, healthy families, and happy marriages. I love to see women fully expressed and sexually, mentally, emotionally, and spiritually fulfilled.

I am *the one*—and *you* are also *the one*.

You have the power to rewrite your story—the story of your family and love, relationships, belonging, communication, and being accepted for who you truly are.

You are *the one* who can learn how to say what feels like the impossible.

You are *the one* who can learn to respond instead of reacting.

You are *the one* who can take down the armor around her heart, and surrender to trust and love within yourself and with others.

You are *the one* who can attract the partner of your dreams.

You are *the one* who creates an unbelievable life and relationships by the juiciness of your pussy and the pleasure you embody—in sex and beyond sex.

You are the creator.

You are *the one* to heal what has been given to you.

You are *the one* who scripts and writes your life and love story.

You are *the one* to be the mother who recognizes her own emotional states and needs and knows they are a priority.

You are *the one* who can love her partner and be a master at the energetic embodiment of who you are.

You are *the one* who is courted like a queen, treated like the prize you are, and satisfied with your deepest desires.

There is nothing you can't experience for yourself because *YOU* are the *one* who has been and still keeps creating it—*all of it*.

Just like *I AM*—and *do*.

Starting Over

Caitlyn Barninger

Caitlyn is a Tampa native with multiple passions centered on education and community. In 2015, she graduated with a bachelor's of science in elementary education from the University of South Florida. Once in the field, she discovered her love for literacy and later went on to receive her master's of education in curriculum and instruction. During her graduate program, she focused heavily on English and writing instruction and participated in the Tampa Bay Area Writing Project, publishing her first children's book with BeaLu Books. Caitlyn has held various roles throughout her career journey from bartender to teacher, executive assistant, and retail leadership. In 2022, she was given the opportunity through her employer Kendra Scott to build relationships with nonprofit organizations in the Tampa Bay and St. Petersburg area.

By taking time to identify her transferable skills, she was able to easily adapt to changes in work environments, and ultimately discover other areas of interest. She hopes her story encourages readers to find the lesson in every experience and move through life with resiliency and grace. She believes that identity does not reside in a job title, but rather who you are in Christ. Despite the many titles she has been given throughout her life, she finds the most fulfillment in being a wife and mom.

———

What do you want to be when you grow up?

I was encouraged to lay forth a destination at the ripe age of five. At best, these proclamations were a way to gauge my ambition, curiosity, and interests. At least, they were a way to foreshadow a future of working positions I felt highly unqualified for, a degree I don't really use, and multiple career pivots, because, well... I was confused.

I found myself wading into the quagmire of insanity that we call adulthood one overpriced coffee at a time. I had finally graduated with a degree in elementary education, and I naively thought teaching would be my lifelong career. After several years of working as a bartender and waitress, I knew I was ready for a "big girl job" (whatever that means).

But sometimes God has other plans.

I technically knew what to expect on my first day in the classroom because I had completed internships in college. I figured doing it on my own should be simple, if not formulaic. I knew there would be challenges because I was hired only two days prior to the first day of school.

What I didn't expect was feeling mentally and emotionally depleted after the first short week. Not from the labor itself, but from pretending that I had it all together. It didn't take long for imposter syndrome to take hold and leave me feeling inadequate, unqualified, and burnt out. There were *many wonderful* things I adored about teaching... I just wasn't ready. It was ultimately not what I wanted to spend my life doing—at least, not in the sense that I had originally anticipated.

So, I turned in my keys to the classroom and went to the gym.

The gym was where I went to escape my problems. Prior to teaching, I had hired a coach and competed in my first bodybuilding bikini competition, and I was hooked. I had fallen in love with the process, the intense focus, and the discipline required to be competitive at that level. In hindsight, the gym was the one place I felt mentally strong.

Now, I was deflated from having walked away from what I wanted so badly and worked so hard to get. I was lost and wandering, and my self-image had crumbled. My coach listened to my grievances about feeling like a failure.

I had no idea what I wanted to do or what step I needed to take next.

The next few months after my hiatus from teaching were dark in comparison to my normal rose-colored perspective. I had experienced heartbreak, death in the family, disordered eating, and an identity crisis as I tried to keep my head above water and my bills paid.

I took a short-term position as a sales representative for a supplement company, thanks to a referral. I didn't know much about the supplement industry (or sales for that matter), but I could make small talk about the gym. So, I spent the next few months supporting a few GNC locations in the Tampa area while trying to get my life together. This point in my life was a true balancing act of numbing my pain with partying and ugly crying in the church parking lot after Sunday service.

Most stores are packed on Black Friday—but apparently, protein and pre-workouts aren't the priority items on people's shopping lists. I was browsing Kate Spade deals online with only a few minutes left of my shift when a strikingly edgy guy with tattoos and piercings walked in wearing a GNC polo.

I met my husband.

Unlike anyone I have ever met, this man has supported my dreams, listened to my big ideas, and encouraged me to rise to opportunities—even when I felt unqualified or afraid.

Eventually, I left the supplement company and went back to hospitality. I enrolled in a graduate program at the University of South Florida to get a master's of education in curriculum and instruction. But not before exploring other interests. After acknowledging that I couldn't endure suffering through another chemistry lecture pretending to be interested, I realized I wanted to lean into my first passion: teaching.

Distressed souls are those who **don't** reflect on what it feels like to yearn for more. They build their empires on the very habits they loathe. They may feel like the walls are closing in but are too enervated and obtuse to change. But a suitable amount of confusion and discontentment are like gasoline on a fire. The heat is there, it just needs a little something to fuel the flame.

When the cloud of despondency clears, the feeling of wandering becomes something to chase. Life becomes a video game. Each challenge becomes a way to earn points, each new endeavor is a level-up.

Starting over becomes the norm instead of something to be evaded.

I had the realization that I did have a passion for teaching, building relationships, communication, and literature. This revelation clicked while I was ruminating on why I enjoyed bartending or teaching in the first place.

I knew everything was about to change once again as I looked down at those little red lines on a positive pregnancy test. In just two years—I became a mom to the most beautiful baby boy I have ever seen, moved across the country to Los Angeles with my little family, and completed my graduate program.

At this point, I had been attending church in Tampa regularly. I wasn't perfect but can say that I handled the changes much more gracefully than I did in my years right after college. In varying degrees of conviction, God began revealing to me that he wasn't interested in my title—He was concerned with my heart. I realized my identity is not found in my circumstances but in Christ.

After a few months in L.A., I went back to work full-time as an executive assistant for the same company that sparked our move to California. I was essentially starting over again, now on a new career path. I realized that skills I had learned in my past positions like my ability to think on my feet and move quickly, edit documents for errors, and network in the office served me in my new role. However, in 2020 everything fell apart along with the rest of society as we knew it.

When we moved back to Tampa, I was starting over once again. I ended up working for another start-up company and then one more after that. I gained confidence in my abilities to figure things out on the fly and realized that many of the skills I learned could be transferrable and valuable to many companies.

I never envisioned myself working in retail. But today, I am an assistant manager for a Kendra Scott store. I have learned quite a bit, especially about retail management and operations within a store and visual merchandising. After about a of year working in the store, I found a new passion in the world of events and philanthropy. Each day I get to work with an amazing group of women and plan philanthropic events that have a positive impact on the community.

Learning to gracefully embrace changes in life and using the transferable skills and knowledge from each endeavor to support the next is one of the most valuable lessons I have ever learned. Each time you pick yourself back up and start again, you gain resiliency and courage. With each milestone, we develop a unique set of skills that somehow intertwine. Each restart inspires new ideas, interests, and goals.

Sometimes you will feel like you are walking through a dark forest with a small flashlight, only seeing the illuminated ground in front of your feet but having no idea what paths are ahead. A truly remarkable moment in life is when you've been walking for so long, trusting in God's plan for your life, and the light starts to shine brighter. You gain a better understanding of who you are and where you are going. When you look back on the path you have traveled, you finally understand *why* you were there in the first place.

My journey certainly isn't over, and change in life is unavoidable—but I hope that my words offer encouragement to women reading this who may feel lost. If this is you, please remember that what you see as failure can be a blessing.

My story isn't special. I am just a woman that had internalized the "pick a career and run with it" mentality that leaves no room for self-exploration, growth, or *grace*. I've felt the agonizing fear of never finding a career that I love, and finally having the freeing realization that what I do for a living does not define me.

And it doesn't define you, either.

The question *what do you want to be when you grow up?*

That's irrelevant... and boring.

The question should really be: *What do you want to do **first**?*

A Passion to Change the World: From Challenging Childhood Expectations to Global Women's Empowerment

Jennifer Stinson

Jennifer Stinson is an Air Force retiree spouse, older sister, aunt, social entrepreneur, unapologetic advocate, stylist, and storyteller leading a life of passion, purpose, and impact. While living in East Asia and exploring the countries of East and Southeast Asia, Jennifer's heart for advocacy for the women and families in these countries burst wide open. She started a purpose-driven business in 2016 in partnership with Noonday Collection to create dignified jobs for women and families living in vulnerable communities of underdeveloped nations, where they use skills that have been passed down for generations.

Jennifer's experiences while stationed in Southwest Asia a few years later only intensified her desire to continue creating meaningful opportunities for others. She could not stifle the passion in her heart that developed the ardent belief that every woman is worthy of a good job, safety, and access to an education. She also believes every family deserves access to dignified jobs at home instead of enduring separation as they provide for their families. Jennifer has a deep fondness for traversing the world and will have explored all seven continents by the end of 2023. She is an ardent scuba diver, ocean torchbearer, and 18-year competitive baton twirler who retired after reaching the pinnacle of her twirling career as a collegiate feature twirler.

A born New Yorker, she was raised in Texas and now resides in the Tampa, Fla., suburbs with her husband and two cats.

You can find her at:

jenniferstinson.co

Facebook: JenniferStinsonNoondayAmbassador

Instagram: jenniferrstinson

LinkedIn: www.linkedin.com/in/jenniferrstinson

As a little girl, I dreamt vividly about my adult life. Becoming a second-grade teacher, just like my elementary school teachers said I would. Marrying a man with a great job and having two children, one boy and one girl. I'd even have a house in the suburbs with a white picket fence and live near my childhood best friend. And, I knew I would see some of the world.

I envisioned myself doing it all by the age of 30.

These dreams flourished amid a childhood filled with activities: dance, Girl Scouts, tennis, learning to play musical instruments—and competitive baton twirling, a sport which I quickly grew to love. Through dedication, perseverance, and training under a strict coach, I won more baton twirling titles at the local, state, regional, and national levels in my 18-year career than I can remember at my now-young age of 50!

While I loved twirling I often missed out on birthday parties and other fun childhood activities because I needed to be at practices, parades, and competitions, which was hard as a child and young adult. While I enjoyed these pursuits, the opportunities came with the weight of the expectation of perfection from my parents in everything I did, from chores to schoolwork to extracurricular activities.

My parents also expected that all things in life be kept extremely private. I was not allowed to talk about my struggles or about things that happened at home. I was once grounded for visiting the elementary school counselor to talk about something that happened at home. That was when I learned that talking about my life outside of the four walls of our home was forbidden. While I can see the long-term effects and struggles I have today as a result of growing up under these immense unrealistic pressures, I recognize my parents also provided goodness in my childhood that helped me develop into the person I am today with a passion to make a difference in the world. They exposed me to travel, shielded me from most of the bad things in the world, consistently pushed me to be successful, and encouraged me to build good character, and my mother made me believe I could be whatever I wanted to be in this life.

After high school, I went to college and pursued degrees in early childhood education and child development and family studies. During this time, I was inducted into Kappa Delta Pi, Honor Society in Education, and Kappa Alpha Theta Fraternity. While there, I was involved in a relationship with a man who mentally, physically, and emotionally abused me; this taught me what I did not want in a life partner. I also no longer dreamt of a career in education and shifted my career focus to the real estate industry. I worked on the administrative side of the real estate industry as a licensed agent while also coordinating the office's monthly charitable arm, a passion I carried with me from my sorority days. I later transferred to serve as vice president of administration for a financial services company and eventually moved back to the world of real estate.

Soon after that, I met my husband online, because where else were early thirtysomethings (the second unexpected development in the childhood dream) supposed to meet quality mates? He was stationed at the Pentagon, and I was living in South Carolina. After spending two-and-a-half years in a successful long-distance relationship, we decided to live in the same town so we could date consistently.

I packed up my cat and moved to my own little place near his new duty station. and we were engaged a few short months later. I already knew he was something extra special because, a year previous to this, when we were still living in separate states, he unexpectedly arrived in town to support me at my niece's funeral, and handled my uncontrollable wailing with grace; she was only two years old at the time.

Shortly after our engagement, we were swept up in a whirlwind of planning a wedding in three months, getting married, going on a honeymoon, packing up our separate homes, and moving to a new duty station together with my cat, which became "our" cat. Our marriage was not just a commitment to each other, it was also a commitment to the government. When the Air Force says it's time to move, you grab the checklist, and each does their part to make it happen by the deadline. They also don't provide white picket fences! I found myself reflecting on how this too was not part of my childhood dream.

Four months after our wedding and our subsequent move, I underwent major back surgery, so trying for children was on hold for most of a year. We were OK with that because we were newlyweds and wanted to enjoy being married for a while before adding an infant into the mix. We told ourselves we would take our time.

Over his career, my husband worked like all our service personnel do, 24-7, 365 days a year (unless they are on leave). I worked my jobs supporting unit functions, sitting on boards, participating in spouse group functions and activities, volunteering, attending base and community functions, taking care of our quarters—and every spouse's favorite agenda item, dealing with maintenance. Along the way, we made friends who have become our family. We also made sure we took our allotted leave (vacation) and started collecting passport stamps.

When we received our assignment for Seoul, South Korea, I was elated. It became my favorite assignment; the people (locals and those we were stationed with), the culture, the food, medical care, and the travel opportunities we were afforded were abundant (this was another part of my childhood dream realized). We still had not gotten pregnant, and when I alerted my gynecologist to my severe pelvic pain, he found heavy endometriosis scarring and active endometriosis through laparoscopic surgery.

A few months later, we met with the reproductive endocrinologist in Seoul, who suggested that because I had a history of endometriosis and polycystic ovary syndrome (that was news to me!) combined with my advanced age of 41, we should start IVF immediately. At that point, I only had a four percent chance of getting pregnant. (Four percent?!)

We had been assigned a mission and like the two competitive people we are, we gathered our support group, prayed a lot, and began. We had two successful cycles with two embryos, but implantation failure. Unfortunately, starting with cycle three, my body just did not want to cooperate anymore. All the years of doctors telling me *you're too young, exercise more, take this*, along with misdiagnoses, had culminated in this. A part of my childhood dream had vaporized.

We explored 13 countries across East and Southeast Asia during our time in South Korea, and they are experiences I will never forget. I walked among people whose first source of employment and livelihood is agriculture, with handiwork (artisan craft) being the second. The people, kindness, the smiles, the food, the culture, the community, and the history all brought me so much joy. But I also experienced heartbreak like I had almost never experienced before. I learned how generational poverty is so difficult to overcome because no jobs pay well enough in safe environments. I saw children fishing, begging, and working in fields to help provide for their families instead of being in school. Although school is free and compulsory up to a certain age—it varies by country—families often do not have the means to afford uniforms, supplies, and transportation.

I learned that girls often marry and have babies before they are adults, and that many women are forced or tricked into exploitation. Families prioritize their sons' schooling because they are expected to be the main breadwinners. Women work at home, then in the fields, then at home, and then at a food cart at night. Even with several generations living under one roof, families struggle to cover the costs of food. It is common for medical care there to only be accessible with cash only, and not necessarily high-quality.

I left our vacation in Cambodia, one of our last in South East Asia, in tears. My heart for advocacy had been awakened, and I wanted to make a difference in places like those we had explored over those three years. I wanted to be a part of the solution for the kinds of poverty and exploitation we saw in places that don't have the resources in place like we do here in the United States.

Two years earlier, a friend had introduced me to an opportunity offered by a socially responsible business that uses fashion to create meaningful opportunities across the globe and believes in the dignity and power of work. This opportunity allowed me to start my own business where I could help end that cycle of poverty. When my husband and I moved back to the United States, I began my journey as a social entrepreneur to make a meaningful impact in the lives of others, advocating for women and families, and alleviating poverty through dignified work.

In 2017, we received an assignment to Southwest Asia. During the next three years I observed tens of thousands (estimated millions in the region) of workers who were separated by thousands of miles from their children and families, frequently for years at a time. They often worked long hours six days a week, many in construction and outdoor environments, just to provide for their families back home. Traveling around South Asia and several countries of Africa, seeing the daily lives of their people, and spending time with artisans in India and Kenya reinforced why I do this work.

When we moved back to the United States at the height of the pandemic, it was my third time in four years starting my business in a new location, this time in the Tampa suburbs. I never gave up!

Even through the challenges of moving and new locations, to date, I have produced enough funding to create four years of artisan jobs and five years of classes for students, all because of sales through my business.

What I have learned over my years of travel and now over seven years as an Independent Noonday Ambassador business owner is that what people in the developing world want most is a good job. Providing dignified, sustainable jobs that pay fair, living wages is lifechanging for them. When they have that, poverty, exploitation, and trafficking are NOT their final story!

I have sat with some of our Artisan Partners in three countries, most recently Guatemala, as well as others from across the globe at our annual conference held in Austin, Texas, and heard their stories of transformation firsthand. They aren't just surviving anymore, they are thriving!

Every single purchase at my trunk shows and website changes lives. Hope. Plans for the future. Dreams. These are three things we all deserve and are providing to those who once never imagined them possible. I advocate and do this work for artisans who finally have sustainable jobs in safe working environments, while keeping their families together. I do it for female coffee growers who now earn fair wages, and for the children and bright young female university-bound scholars who now have education opportunities through our scholarship initiatives. I do it to work against the evils of modern-day slavery.

But there is still work to be done. The pandemic pushed one hundred million people in the developing world back into extreme poverty and twenty million girls may never step foot back into the classroom. These are devastating statistics.

The artisans depend on me, and I depend on them. I count on women, men, and business owners to partner with me to help lift women and families around the world out of poverty through trunk shows where the power of your purchases can change the trajectory of lives for people who need dignified opportunities.

I do this work for me. I'm so grateful for the opportunity to make a positive global impact and support my local community through gorgeous fair trade accessories and delicious coffee. We get a chance to "wear *their* story" and "share *their* story."

We Attract the Lives We Believe In

Alexandra Valencia

Alexandra is a seasoned full-time realtor who has served the Tampa Bay Area for over six years. Her dynamic journey has seen her representing a diverse clientele that includes buyers, sellers, and investors. However, her true passion lies in guiding and supporting first-time homebuyers on their path to homeownership.

With a commitment to education, empowerment, and building meaningful relationships, Alexandra has built the foundation of her career. She believes that helping the next generation of homeowners make informed decisions is not just a job but a calling. By assisting them in acquiring their first homes, she contributes to their financial stability and future prosperity.

When she's not assisting clients in navigating the real estate market, Alexandra enjoys the laid-back lifestyle of Tampa Bay with her husband. They share a love for adventure and are often fishing, surfing, or eating.

———

I have lived *many* lives, each of which has paved the way to where I am now.

From my early struggles with trauma and addiction to traveling the world alone to moving across the country to chase love to multiple failed attempts at new businesses, each chapter made me into the badass woman I am today. Even writing this is another stepping stone for the woman I am creating for tomorrow. After 34 years of experience, I have learned there are good days, and there are learning days.

I figure as long as I do my best and don't kill anyone, I'm usually heading in the right direction.

It wasn't until I learned that happiness is a decision, and no one owes me anything that I began to grow. You can either sit in it or get with it—but the world isn't going to wait for you.

My teen years were a mix of teenage angst and some heavy family trauma. I lost three family members including my brother Anthony in the span of six months. Losing Anthony blew out the light in my heart. I didn't know how to deal, nor did my parents. He was our everything. Anthony was disabled and lived with cerebral palsy since birth. He could not walk, talk, or feed himself—but damn, did he light up a room with his smile. He was the purest, most beautiful human I have ever had the privilege of knowing. Everyone gravitated towards him; I and many others felt like we were better humans for having known him.

After losing Anthony, we all turned to our own vices. Substance abuse and the wreckage it brings with it took over my life from age 12 to 19. It wasn't a long period of time, but I went down fast. In the end, I was suicidal, addicted, and broken. My family had done the best they could, but they were learning how to live after this trauma as well. I cannot thank my parents enough for doing the hard things. At 17, I came to a crossroads, so I started going to 12-step meetings. It took about three years of relapsing for me to finally get the message, but I eventually surrendered.

Thankfully, my parents had found me the most incredible counselor on the planet. With their support, meetings, and my higher power, I stayed clean and sober for over 10 years.

In that 10-year span, I grew up a lot, but my path was a little less traditional. Now that I had burned most of my bridges as far as school, friends, and relationships, I had to start fresh. I had my own apartment at 17 and was always able to hold on to one or two jobs. I knew how to hustle like my parents, and I knew how to talk to people. I learned how to connect with like-minded people who wanted to grow and do better. I believe that you are the company you keep, so you should be sure to surround yourself with people who expand your mind and your heart.

When I turned 20, I was working for the same city I grew up in, within a department that typically required a degree. Since I never finished college, it was odd when my friends started to come home without their promised careers, and here I was, already making great money. They would ask how I got there, to which I could only say, "I worked hard and networked with the right people." It proved to me that what I was doing was working, and I could grow. But over a few years, I became depressed. I quickly found out that corporate America was not for me, and that I was too young to work a nine-to-five job with only weekends to find joy.

I had done well for myself on paper, but I had no desire to live that life. I felt like I had outgrown my surroundings. I began resenting others, I was unhealthy, I had no spark. In desperation (or as I would now call it, *alignment*), I called one of my oldest friends who had moved away for advice. After a three-hour phone call and many "why nots," I had a one-way ticket to Hawaii.

I broke up with my guy, sold the belongings, quit the job, and ALOHA!

What's funny about that happening at age 23 is that I felt something in me for a long time that "23" would be my year. And it was. It was the birth of a new me. It woke up my soul and rocked me to my core. I had outgrown where I had been, and living in a new environment helped me bloom. I met so many incredible people who were doing what I craved. Traveling, surfing, living healthy, community. They spoke the language I desired to learn and showed me the ropes. I landed a job in a restaurant so that if I ever moved again, I could always get a job. I bartended, served, and worked at hotels and small businesses. I learned how to network through my guests and met many wonderful people. It was a magical time, and I am so grateful that the islands welcomed me in.

Hawaii is an incredible place, and deeply spiritual. I have so much respect for the people and the culture. I had my spiritual awakening, and I felt more alive than ever. It was time for a new adventure, my next thrill. So I figured, why not do some traveling?

I went to Thailand and Indonesia alone and was there for a little over three months. I quickly learned that "traveling" and "vacation" are two different things. In the months I was gone, I was robbed, in a motor accident, and hospitalized for sickness. I wanted an adventure, and I got it. I had to have faith that I would be taken care of, believe that I was capable and that this would all make a great story one day.

If I were to write my headstone now, I'd include something about how important it is to travel. Get out of your comfort zone, challenge yourself, meet new people, learn about new customs and cultures. Traveling alone gave me the biggest confidence boost I have ever had in my entire life.

I figured *nothing* could rattle me after that—and I was here for it. How could life get *any* better? Enter, a new (manifested) relationship.

I said once that I would never move for a man, but when he's 6'4 and looks like Patrick Dempsey, you follow the man. This was how I landed in Florida, where my now husband Patrick was born and raised. The universe brought us together while surfing, and I still get giddy over the romantics of it all. Where we lived at the time was a little too far to make new friends and find a career, so when I decided to pursue a career in real estate, I followed the money. Insert Tampa Bay. I got a job at a high-end restaurant where I could make solid tips and meet professionals and locals. I got another job at a fitness store so I could meet like-minded people and get back into a healthier lifestyle.

I knew the steps I needed to take before I ever hung my license: Create a community, get involved, and be seen.

The best catalyst was someone telling me that they didn't think I would find success in real estate and that maybe I should find a salaried job instead. (I had already learned that lesson.) If you ever want to see me fly, just tell me that I can't do something! Once my license was hung, it took all but one year for me to be recognized as one of the top 15 percent of Coldwell Banker® realtors, and each year I continue to be recognized for my accomplishments. More importantly, I was able to create a clientele base of like-minded people. I became intentional with my marketing, showed up authentically online, and connected with those who I felt were my people.

Since day one, I have started every day with intention. I read, I journal, I wake up two hours before I need to be anywhere. I work out four to six days a week. I set hours for my business. I show up to the office. I make it a point to meet and work with agents I like. I travel for business, and I show the universe I am here and I am ready to do what needs to be done. People over profit, always.

Every day is different in my career, but my intentions stay the same: I take care of myself first, then I take care of others. If there is no "me," there is no "us" — and I believe that is what a lot of people are missing in their lives, that work-life balance. For me, as much as having a routine sounds boring, I thrive. I know what works for me, and I do not change the formula. Real estate is as exciting as it is terrifying. You handle one of the most expensive, life-altering decisions people make. I don't believe this is a career you can do halfway — and I believe you are doing your clients a disservice if you are.

I can't do anything halfway and expect to succeed.

Over the years, the learning days have choked me up less and less, and the wins have gotten bigger. I always remind myself that as long as my friends and family are safe and healthy, everything else will work itself out.

At the end of the day, if my side of the street is clean and I can come home to my husband, it's a great day.

We Can't Be Defined

Lora Van Balen

Lora Van Balen is an accomplished marketing manager for California Closets Tampa Bay and is highly skilled in her field. She is driven by her passion for creating meaningful connections with people through her work.

Lora's work at California Closets Tampa Bay is a testament to her dedication, creativity, and unwavering commitment to excellence. She has made remarkable contributions to the franchise's growth by consistently finding new ways to develop her expertise in interior design, logistics, budgeting, conflict resolution, and leadership.

She has achieved a lot in her career, including creating and hosting the Home & Design Solutions Podcast on iHeartRadio. By seamlessly integrating her creativity with the home and design industry, she has created innovative and effective marketing campaigns that have made remarkable contributions to the franchise's growth.

Lora is not just a marketer; she's a community advocate, a brand ambassador, and a passionate storyteller. She captures the hearts and minds of Tampa's community by being a determined, outgoing, confident, compassionate, creative risk-taker who dares to dream big. Her passion lies in creating meaningful connections with people through her work.

Additionally, Lora is an advocate for the community and a passionate supporter of empowering women and future leaders. Her ongoing work with Girls Inc. and Dress for Success is a testament to her dedication, creativity, and unwavering commitment to empowering the women and future leaders of Tampa Bay.

―――

I've spent over six years at California Closets in Tampa Bay, working alongside some incredibly talented people. My colleagues and mentors have inspired me with their creativity and innovation.

As the acting brand ambassador for the past four years, I have played a crucial role in significantly growing our franchise. Despite the challenges posed by COVID-19, I doubled our leads and revenue. I achieved noteworthy results by securing three distinctive sponsorships with prominent media outlets such as Daytime TV, Great Day Live, and iHeartRadio's Mix100.7.

Moreover, I accomplished the opening of a new showroom location, which was a significant milestone for the company. Through diligent effort and strategic planning, I successfully executed marketing campaigns that effectively reached and resonated with our intended audiences across various media platforms. As a result of my dedication, my work has garnered numerous accolades and awards at both the local and national levels.

I've been recognized as One to Watch by the Tampa Bay Builders Association and won their Best Overall Marketing Campaign award twice. It is my responsibility to develop and implement innovative marketing campaigns that effectively capture the attention of our customers. Once the opportunities have been identified, I create campaigns tailored to our target audience's needs and preferences. These are designed to engage customers and make a lasting impression, ultimately driving sales and revenue growth. Through careful planning, execution, and evaluation, I ensure that our marketing campaigns are effective, efficient, and aligned with our overall business objectives.

I believe humor and wit are paramount in making content engaging and relatable. I take great pride in my ability to blend data-driven insights with clever humor to create content that truly resonates with my audience. Throughout my career, I have honed my unique talent in combining data and spirit, and I continue to strive for excellence in everything I do.

Marketing and creating are my true calling. From the beginning, I have felt an intense passion for these fields that has only grown stronger with time. These areas allow me to utilize my innate abilities to communicate, persuade, and connect with people, which are appreciated and essential for success. The more I delved into the intricacies of marketing, the more I realized that it was a perfect fit for me. The blend of creativity, strategy, and human psychology it required resonated deeply with me. It was like a puzzle I couldn't wait to solve, and every new challenge only fueled my love for it even more. (I'm a BIG stats gal.)

Growing up in Northern Virginia, I always knew I was a beach girl at heart. I inherited my father's knack for construction, DIY, power tools, and home projects from a young age. I find creative outlets in everything I do, which I attribute to being left-handed. I studied biochemistry in college but excelled unexpectedly in honors Shakespeare and psychology courses. I completed community college with only a general science associate degree.

As a child, I was affectionately known as 'Princess Lora' by my father, who always found my aversion to compliments about my appearance amusing. Over the years, this nickname has come to symbolize my life's journey, through its highs and lows, triumphs, and challenges. Although societal norms often dictate that we conform to specific standards in our appearance, behavior, and attitude, I have always been determined to carve my own path and embrace the unconventional. I am grateful for my adventurous spirit and the way it has shaped me into the person I am today.

I used to care about being popular and fitting in, striving for perfection. But now, I celebrate both my "princess" and "weirdo" sides, recognizing them as strengths. I firmly believe in self-awareness and personal growth, always pushing myself to be better. As the saying goes, "A shark that stops swimming drowns."

I've lived a life full of adventure and diverse experiences before finding my true calling. From tackling opponents on the rugby field to serving drinks for a flashy corporation, from strutting my stuff in beauty pageants to being a ring girl, and even braving the waves while surfing and snowboarding (despite my tendency to get hurt), I've never shied away from embracing my individuality. When someone doubts me, I channel my 5'3" and 115-pound frame into proving them wrong. And you know what? That underdog spirit has helped me carve out my own path in life. There's something about being underestimated that makes the journey even more thrilling (*wink).

Having developed a minor social media presence before moving to Florida, I had an audience but no purpose. My career was an accidental discovery that came about through what I often refer to as "running my mouth." I have always been a natural conversationalist, someone who could engage with anyone about anything. This ability to communicate effectively and passionately, often without a filter, was something about my personality that at times has been perceived as a threat in the corporate environment. However, as fate would have it, this talent of mine inadvertently led me into the ever-evolving world of marketing. Through my creativity, strategic thinking, and skill of running my mouth, I have become a successful woman in my industry, and I hope to inspire others with my achievements.

As a woman, I have always believed in the power of authenticity. I refuse to be defined by the societal norms imposed upon us. Instead, I choose to embrace my uniqueness and individuality, even if it means being labeled as "weird," "different," or "eccentric." These adjectives may be associated with my character, but they do not define me. I am so much more than that. I am a force to be reckoned with. I am ambitious, tenacious, and cunning. I have a facetious sense of humor that keeps me grounded and a manipulative streak that helps me get things done. But don't be fooled by my abrasive exterior—I am fiercely loyal and deeply compassionate.

I have many passions as a creative director, writer, photographer, editor, publisher, director, moment maker, and fashion enthusiast. Unlike a traditional nine-to-five job, I work according to my own schedule, which I like to call 8-Fate. I take pride in representing both my personal and professional brands in every aspect of my life. My unique quality is that I am different from others, and I embrace my quirks and idiosyncrasies because they make me who I am. I firmly believe that with the right attitude and determination, anything is possible. As Marie Forleo aptly puts it, "Everything is figureoutable."

Of course, I am not perfect. Sometimes I am a self-proclaimed "hot mess in a sundress." But even in my messiest moments, I am still slaying. Because that's just who I am: a powerful woman who refuses to be defined by anyone else's standards. As I reflect on my personal journey, I can't help but see myself as a shark—a creature that never stops moving forward, no matter what obstacles lie in its path. To keep my momentum going, I constantly nourish myself with knowledge and seek out new ways to sharpen my skills and navigate the unpredictable waters of life. While there's no one-size-fits-all guidebook for success, I firmly believe that consuming knowledge is the key to carving out your own path and achieving your goals.

By maintaining a clear sense of purpose and taking care of both my physical and mental well-being, I'm able to stay focused, driven, and energized, no matter what challenges come my way. And with this mindset, I know that anything and everything is within my grasp.

With absolutely no formal background in marketing, I have still established authority and expertise in my field. If you had asked me six years ago how I did it, I would say: The key to slaying any project, large or small, is to plan for the best, expect the worst, and persevere through every hardship and struggle of everyday life. Hey, if it was easy, everyone could do it! Sometimes you have to be creative in your problem-solving and be innovative with that outside-the-box way of thinking.

Remember, one size does not fit all. Tackle each obstacle individually, and you will have a fabulous outcome.

Life is beautiful because the past only gives us the wisdom to make better choices based on our experiences, it does not dictate our present or future. We have the power to pave our path. I don't usually conform to people's expectations of who I should be. Categories do not limit us; we can play multiple roles and achieve anything we set our minds to.

I'm sharing my philosophy with you in the hope that you find it insightful and inspiring. I urge you to join the "Slaying" movement, which aims to break the glass ceiling for women everywhere. With your support, women everywhere can achieve their goals. This message may seem brief, but it comes from a place of passion and dedication. So, let's work together to empower women and create a more equitable world for all.

I really do believe in the slogan, "Gals help gals make new pals!"

Thank you for your time reading my chapter. Cheers!

Who Knew You Could Improve Your Life without Leaving Your Bed?

Jenna Schwartz

Jenna Schwartz is a master connector, who uses her ability to bring together like-minded individuals and create countless deals and deep relationships. As co-director for Tampa's Boss Talks, Jenna leads and moderates events with intent to empower and mentor attendees. Jenna prides herself on giving back, leading her to co-found a charity and sit on various committees for The Spring of Tampa Bay, both charities that aim to increase awareness of domestic violence and aid those impacted by it.

Additionally, Jenna is a co-founder, board member, and chief experience officer of Tampa Entrepreneurs. Outside of her personal endeavors, Jenna is a force in the business world as a founding member of the Provenance Consulting Group, an executive coaching consulting firm, co-author of the book *Dream Big Do Bigger,* and buy-side associate partner for the M&A Advisory firm Stoneridge Partners. Jenna's background also includes a decade of health IT experience, sales, and marketing. With a passion for bringing value and positively impacting those around her, Jenna captivates and encourages her audience to take action.

———

Look, Mom and Dad... I did it! I got an A!

Growing up, I was always greeted by *good jobs*, congratulations, and a spot on the fridge. The validation was intoxicating and became a drug. Whether it was a parent, friend, boss, or significant other, their validation was the barometer of my value. But the sickening feeling that washed over me whenever I disappointed another person was so significant that I spent the first 28 years of my life in a cycle of people-pleasing and niceties. The results were anxiety, depression, lack of fulfillment, and staying in environments that didn't serve me.

If you resonate with any of these emotions, I hope that this chapter can open your mind to an adapted perspective enabling you a pathway forward to more internal peace and fulfillment in life.

Before sharing my story, I must prepare you: the road to success will look different for everyone, just as the definition of success in and of itself varies from person to person. For simplicity, think about a cake (or a dessert you enjoy): there are thousands of variations and recipes to make a cake and (objectively speaking) thousands of delicious cakes. I find that many productivity journals, self-help materials, podcasts, and those types of things give a specific set of directions, a recipe, for success. Each human is unique and must develop a recipe that works for their own path. Still, there are commonalities in these thousands of recipes that make a cake a cake. Otherwise, every dish would be called a variation of a cake.

With that, let's explore how to apply 12 steps to your unique variations and dive in together!

In this section, get ready for a myriad of quotes. They say "misery loves company," and lying in bed with Instagram... well that was my company. Hours of scrolling through other people's airbrushed lives bred the cycle of my depression, and I would count the minutes until I could go to sleep. It felt like living was excruciating. When Instagram's algorithm began to lean more towards inspirational content, I began aching for this promised livelihood. I lay there in my misery and frankly didn't do a damn thing about it—well, not right away anyhow. I was addicted to my identity and the fear of change made any change inconceivable.

Then I began to believe one of those Instagram quotes, "One's ability to grow is directly proportional to one's ability to look at oneself in the mirror."

Ooof, that stung. I was hit with a big realization: Was I the common denominator in my misery? Was I not a victim of the world but, instead, my own villain?

Unbeknownst to me at the time, I had been hobbling along my own version of a 12-step program, and it seemed like I had just processed through the first five steps: awareness, acknowledgment, getting honest, open-mindedness, and taking personal responsibility.

Did that mean I was already just over 40% closer to inner peace, and I didn't even have to leave my bed?

By this point, I was forced up and out of the comfort of my denial blanket. It became clear there were only two options:

1) *Change NOTHING and stay addicted to my depression, barely making it through each day; or*
2) *Change something, ANYTHING, that could get me out of this mindset!*

This brings us to the next three steps: *willingness, trust, and faith.* I was desperate to be happy and find a willingness to try just about any resource thrown my way. Traditional talk therapy, psychiatry, breathwork, mindset coaching, tarot card reading, acupuncture, daily gratitude practice, and more. Day-to-day nothing seemed to change, yet the desperation to be happier drove my ability to begin to trust and have faith in any of these methods.

Looking back, it seemed that the ability to be brainwashed and in denial of my misery was the same strength that "brainwashed" me into believing in my success. While, initially this chapter wasn't meant to highlight a 12-step program, as I began to share my story, I began to see the parallels.

To all my people-pleasers out there, it's likely you know we need to keep pushing through only being 67% of the way through the program.

I found the final steps to be the trickiest yet found them co-mingling with everything along the journey: humility, tolerance, forgiveness, and love. However, it seemed I could manage most of these steps while back in bed too, thankfully as it was a blessing the days I could get out of bed. I began shifting my self-talk and mantras.

My natural internal thoughts went something like this:

"Why me?"

"It's not fair!"

"I hate that I feel so deeply, and others don't."

"I hate being me."

And I remember the moment I realized, *oof... I am my own villain.* Looks like my thoughts were doing a great job of reminding me how awful my life was and being my own bully.

The mantras then shifted to:

"I am so grateful to be able to feel so deeply and get to feel passion deeper than so many others."

"I am so grateful I have a heart and that I'm not a psychopath and not living a life in "prison."* (*Author note: Yes, I really would think about how if I had no heart I could be a horrible human and end up living in a cement cell and how much of a blessing I had.)

Even as I would silently cry myself to sleep, I would say these mantras and similar ones, focusing on forgiving and loving who I am until I fell asleep, and you know what happened? After only a few days I could feel the magic beginning to unfold. I began brainwashing myself into being a positive person who loves herself! And I naturally began choosing more fulfilling opportunities and adapting my definition of acceptable behaviors from those who stayed in my life.

So, here are the 12 steps, as I lived them for myself:

Step 1: Identify and cultivate *awareness* of wanting "something" to be different. For me, that feeling was wanting to get to a promised land of "more."

Step 2: *Acknowledge* your desire. I defined "more" as getting through a day happily.

Step 3: *Get honest* with yourself. It takes courage to look in the mirror and be real with ourselves.

Step 4: Be *open-minded.* This means a willingness to hear and learn. I was willing to try just about anything to feel better.

Step 5: *Take personal responsibility.* Throw out the excuses. I had to own the fact I was addicted to my identity and was getting in my own way.

Step 6: Be *willing* to change. This is the action you take relative to your open-mindedness. In my example, I gave it my all via breathwork, mindset coaching, therapy, and more.

Step 7: *Trust the process.* This is critical because you must believe in a desire you have yet to achieve or reach. For me, this looked like trusting each of my resources.

Step 8: *Have faith.* You must believe that you will achieve that desire. For some, this may look like trusting a high power.

Step 9: Practice *acceptance.* Accepting the process requires humility, and you can expect a humbling experience.

Step 10: *Have patience.* They say Rome wasn't built in a day, nor is true change. Expect to have your tolerance tested for the speed you move through your process. In my example, the overall process took close to a year to go from my lowest point to happy—at least, on most days. This is always a work in progress.

Step 11: *Practice forgiveness.* The ability to forgive oneself can be one of the most challenging steps. For me, it took repeating the same mantras over and over. Early on, saying the mantras helped me trust, have faith, and practice tolerance, and eventually, they helped me forgive myself.

And lastly...

Step 12: *Love yourself.* The final step is the byproduct of all the steps above. Remember that small consistent actions are transformative, enabling you to reach your heart's desires and live a life of fulfillment.

The Power of Self Perception

Bria Patti

Bria Patti, a proud Tampa Bay native, stands as an exceptional residential real estate agent with RE/MAX Champions. Since obtaining her license in 2017, Bria has consistently demonstrated a commitment to guiding families and investors throughout Tampa Bay toward their real estate goals.

Rooted in a track record that speaks for itself, Bria's professional journey is fueled by a passion for client success and satisfaction. She is committed to listening to her clients' needs, utilizing her strong negotiating skills, and leveraging her extensive network to ensure a successful and seamless transaction. Bria's aspirations extend far beyond the realm of real estate. As the co-director of Boss Talks Tampa, an influential networking and mentorship platform, she is an advocate for empowering women business owners and professionals. Bria's involvement in various women's professional groups, nonprofits, and The Tampa Entrepreneurs Group underlines her commitment to both her craft and the community she holds dear.

When she's not selling real estate or attending events, Bria loves to enjoy all that Tampa has to offer. Some of her simple pleasures include walking down Iconic Bayshore Blvd, cooking for her friends, and spending quality time with her rescue dog Brady. When you choose Bria Patti as your real estate agent, you're not just partnering with another realtor, you're working with someone who genuinely cares about you and your needs, who will work endlessly for you, and who believes the relationship should extend beyond the closing table.

———

Perspective is a unique lens through which we view the world, in line with the saying, "One man's trash is another man's treasure."

It's all about how we choose to perceive things. While we may not always have control over our circumstances, we certainly have control over how we interpret them. This concept has deeply resonated with me, as I've often found myself in situations beyond my control, which initially appeared as weaknesses or disadvantages. However, I've learned to shift my perspective and transform these challenges into sources of strength.

In March 2017, at the age of 20, I took a leap of faith by obtaining my real estate license. To my surprise, I passed the real estate exam on my first attempt, thanks to the sharpness of my youthful mind and the study skills I had honed during college. In that pivotal moment, it became clear to me that real estate was my calling. Despite living in my parents' home and lacking a concrete life plan, I jumped into the world of running my own business.

Many, including myself at times, questioned the wisdom of my decision to dive headfirst into the real estate world at such a young age.

Society often dictates that success is achieved through obtaining a degree, working a nine-to-five job, and steadily climbing the corporate ladder—at least, this is an expectation imposed on teenagers and young adults. However, I was determined to break the mold and exceed conventional expectations.

Being in an office where everyone was double or even triple my age was undeniably intimidating. I often found myself unintentionally belittled, perceived more as a child than a professional eager to cultivate a career. However, as I became more educated in real estate and grew more confident in my unique contributions, I came to realize that I deserved a seat at the table. While I may have lacked years of experience, I brought a fresh and creative perspective and a tech-savvy mindset. I was not "set in old ways"; instead, I was able to swiftly acquire new skills and adapt to change—a trait I observed to be challenging for many of my colleagues.

Age became a persistent source of concern for me during those initial years. I often felt like I resembled a child rather than a capable professional ready to sell someone's home. When I went to meet older clients, their first question would inevitably be, "You look so young. How old are you?" Answering that question filled me with anxiety, fearing that they might not take me seriously. Some praised my youthful determination, while others held preconceived notions about the abilities of young adults. Unfortunately, there were instances when I lost potential clients because of their reservations about my age. There were even plenty of times that I would face this judgment upon meeting other agents for the first time. Eventually, I reached a point where I had to confront this issue head-on. Should I allow my age to define me and impede my passion, or could I find a way to transform perceptions of youth into a genuine advantage for my clients?

I chose the latter. Thanks to the help and support of my friends, family, and mentors, I shifted the narrative surrounding someone in their early twenties. Now, when faced with objections about my age, I respond with confidence because I recognize why it's beneficial to hire me: I don't have children, so I'm available even in the evenings; I'm tech-savvy and adaptable; I prioritize providing dedicated service; I'm willing to travel all around Tampa Bay for you; and I'm exceptionally efficient because I treat my business as my child.

Once I stopped allowing my age to limit me and I gained the self-assurance I needed, I began to flourish, and that haunting question—both in my head and from people approaching me—seemed to decrease.

As cliché as it may sound, you can't alter time. I couldn't hop into a time machine and instantly become the older, wiser version of myself I aspired to be in those moments. Instead, I focused on changing the way people perceived me. I did some self-reflection and worked on boosting my confidence, nurturing self-love, and educating myself about real estate. I also took deliberate steps to place myself in environments where I could learn from those I admired.

At just 21, I proudly represented one of my previous brokerages in the Chamber of Commerce, attended numerous networking events, and even became a vendor at local events to get more comfortable talking about real estate with people of all ages. Throughout my life, I've often been told that I possess a maturity beyond my years. I've had the ability to engage in meaningful conversations with individuals older than me. Making the choice to overcome the fear and shift my thoughts was a vital tool to succeed. Easier said than done, I know, but shifting one's perspective is a potent tool for breaking out of your comfort zone and fostering personal growth.

I have witnessed a notable shift in the societal perception of women in recent times. We have made significant strides in altering the traditional notions of what it means to be a woman and the contributions we make in the business world. Women bring a unique perspective, a different way of thinking, and a deep sense of empathy to the workforce—a powerful combination that sets us apart from others and enhances the professional environment. Helping other women learn from this shift and step into their power is incredibly important to me. I'm an active member of several women's networking groups here in Tampa, and I'm fortunate to serve as the co-director of the Tampa chapter of a national women's mentorship and networking organization called Boss Talks.

It's a truly fulfilling experience to bring like-minded women together, fostering support for each other's businesses, lifting one another up, and engaging in meaningful conversations to build strong connections. Interestingly, I didn't actively seek the role of co-director. My friend Jenna, who is also featured in this book, initially held the position. I attended her events but never thought I would be in a position to host. She saw something in me that I hadn't recognized myself—my dedication to marketing her events on my social media, bringing new members to the group, assisting with event setups, and offering genuine support. While I viewed these actions as simply being a supportive friend, Jenna saw leadership qualities in me. She encouraged me to change my perspective and recognize it for what it truly was. She helped me cultivate a passion for helping other women, which I'm forever grateful for. I am honored to share the director role with such an amazing and powerful woman.

As I've matured, I've come to realize the importance of having friends or individuals in your corner who can help you recognize and cultivate qualities within yourself that might not be immediately evident and support you in nurturing and embodying those qualities. When you find people like that, keep them; they didn't get put in your life for nothing.

Learning to shift one's perspective is an ongoing and often challenging task. It's not always straightforward to identify the positive aspects of a situation and take action to change our mindset. However, the ability and willingness to step back, engage in self-reflection, and recognize our strengths is a truly powerful tool for personal growth. I strive to apply this principle in various aspects of my life, including all types of relationships, business endeavors, and when facing my own internal battles. I challenge you to delve deep within yourself and identify a persistent objection, struggle, or situation you're currently facing.

Reflect on how it makes you feel in its current state, and then imagine the transformative power of turning it into a source of positivity or strength. Consider the small changes you can make today to shift your current situation in a positive direction. It's a privilege to share my story with you, and I genuinely hope it can inspire you to reevaluate your life and circumstances. My goal is to empower you to unlock the ability to change your perspective and uncover the positive aspects of life.

My Life Reimagined: From Emotional Scars to Empowered Success

Anita Arrendondo

Anita Arredondo, the CEO and founder of Be Healthy Weight Loss and Wellness, stands as a shining light of inspiration throughout the vibrant city of Tampa, Fla. Her life's narrative is a testament to resilience and true commitment to the cause of health and wellness.

Anita's remarkable journey is defined by her battles against two life-threatening adversaries: melanoma and breast cancer. She embodies the spirit of a warrior, emerging stronger and more determined after each encounter. Her personal struggles have kindled a deep well of compassion, compelling her to make a profound impact on the lives of others.

As the driving force behind Be Healthy, Anita has crafted a platform that provides vital resources, guidance, and priceless support to individuals on their wellness journeys. She is not merely a survivor; she is a relentless advocate, empowering individuals to take charge of their well-being.

Beyond her professional accolades, Anita is a dedicated mother, wife, and grandmother, balancing her entrepreneurial pursuits with the joys and challenges of family life. Her ability to harmonize career success with personal fulfillment underscores her exceptional leadership skills and devotion to her loved ones.

Anita's narrative is nothing short of extraordinary, a testament to the power of determination and grit to create positive change. From cancer survivor to the driving force behind Be Healthy, her story inspires and offers hope to those facing their own trials, reminding all that no obstacle is insurmountable and that strength resides within us to conquer even the most formidable challenges.

———

You know the old saying, "When you make plans, God laughs"?

I feel like I am walking proof of that—and have been for most of my adult life. Not in a bad way, more in that trusting-the-process-however-difficult-it-might-be   and   should-come-more-easily-to-me-at-this-point way.

Does it ever get easier? Nope. But I like to believe I am getting better as I get older.

I have always believed in happily ever after, but sometimes, it hasn't felt like it believed in me. When I was 18, I thought I was going to have it all. I fell HARD for my older daughter's father, who would be one of the first almost impossible lessons I had to learn.

He was seven years my senior, which probably should have been a warning sign. He repeatedly asked me to marry him, promising that I could continue to pursue my dreams of being a nurse.

He promised me the world, but that isn't what he delivered. That lie is hard to type even now.

What I received was years of abuse. There was no nursing school or any kind of school until I decided to enroll against his approval. He made it impossible for me to keep up with the school workload, between caring for our young daughter, working, and attempting to study. It became very apparent immediately he did not plan on supporting me at all. I was expected to work full-time, care for an infant, be a housewife, and keep up with my schoolwork if that is what I chose to do. Sound unthinkable? It was.

His game was control, through whatever means necessary, whether it be comments about how fat and ugly I was or that I was nothing without him. When you hear things like this enough, you start to believe it. It becomes a part of you that is VERY hard to shed.

Luckily, I was stubborn enough to try anyway. I attended the classes. With every class I took, I felt smarter, more empowered, more courageous. More like *me*.

As every story goes, there came the breaking point. One night, things turned physical, and I couldn't take it anymore. I left with my two-year-old daughter under one arm and a laundry basket under the other, determined that this wasn't going to be my life any longer.

That turning point brought more abuse, both by his family and him, but I knew I couldn't continue to raise my daughter in that kind of abusive household. Every name he called me, every attempt at controlling me, to make me feel weak and small, only served to make me stronger. While I struggled to support my daughter, I was able to make ends meet with the help and love of my amazing mother and stepfather. I know I wouldn't have made it without them.

Although things were tough, I never gave up on meeting the man my daughter and I deserved. I met the love of my life, and soulmate, my now-husband Tony, on a dating app when I was 32. I didn't know someone could make you feel like the only one in the room, but that is what Tony does for me. I felt like I had met my Prince Charming, and I was *finally* going to get that fairytale ending.

That's not how real life works though, is it?

We wanted desperately to add one more to our family. While we were able to conceive twice, both resulted in miscarriages. This is one of those times that, while it felt like God was laughing at me, I knew He was making me stronger, however unfair it felt at the time. During this time, I was in a horrific car accident that I still have aftereffects from years later. I shut down. Tony and I gave up on our dream and once again, God had other plans.

It was then that our youngest, our rainbow baby, was conceived. We were beyond thrilled, and our family was complete.

When my youngest was two months shy of turning two, and my eldest almost 13, my mother, my best friend and lifeline, died suddenly. This last piece is the one that almost did me in. I had weathered everything else, but I didn't know how to go on without her. I had to be strong and carry on without the person that had always been there for me. As a struggling new mom, I threw myself into caring for everyone else, effectively losing myself in the process.

I found my passion working as a health coach at a local diet center. I was in love. I wanted to help everyone and do all the things. I have always loved to teach and had tried to complete my master's degree in teaching after my mother died. It left me feeling flat and unfulfilled. But this... *this* was something else! Coaching adults and teaching them about their bodies was a dream come true. I saw the opportunity to make a huge difference for these people, and I wanted *more*.

Maybe the Universe or God knew I was avoiding taking proper care of myself because while I threw myself into helping others take charge of their health, mine took a sharp decline. I was diagnosed first with malignant melanoma and then, a year later, stage 2 invasive lobular carcinoma—breast cancer, every woman's worst nightmare.

Tony, my knight in shining armor, sat me down and informed me, "You have two minutes to have your pity party, but then you have to pull your big girl panties up and fight like the badass woman I married." I took those two minutes, but after, I fought like hell, through a year of chemo, double mastectomy, and multiple reconstructive surgeries. As of this book's publishing, I am a 12-year-strong survivor, but the story doesn't end there.

The medications, surgeries, and just trying to keep going took a major toll. I gained weight and became very unhealthy. I remember the realization that I wasn't living, just keeping my head down. I didn't want to just survive. I wanted to *thrive*. I dug in and started to apply the tools that I learned as a health coach to myself. I became my own client and not only lost the weight but turned my health and mindset completely around.

When you are ready for the opportunity, God will plop it right in front of you. But you must make sure you are looking for it. The Affirmations Project was that opportunity for me. The project has a mission to support survivors and educate us, teaching that we are not our scars. We are not the illness. Their mission of self-love resonated with me, and I agreed to have my body painted, for all to see. A symbol of my healing, my strength, and my hope and that I was still here. I still mattered. The word that I chose to have painted across my chest was *stronger* because that is what these experiences did for me. It made me stronger than I ever could have imagined.

I had a choice. I could survive or I could live, and I chose to LIVE. I launched Be Healthy Weight Loss and Wellness and became a certified nutrition coach to create a safe, non-judgmental space, where people can learn how to live a healthy lifestyle *and* love their body, not just diet. This is a community of supportive, caring, educated coaches who help others *thrive*.

This business is based on two beliefs: first, that you can be healthy AND happy; second, that coaches who are ready to make a difference can work from anywhere to create that ripple effect. My company is set up to offer opportunities for our coaches to build a life that fits their needs and work around their schedules.

I did it that way on purpose. There was nothing out there like this when I was a broke single mom. I did it for the woman I used to be.

I think about that girl a lot. I know how proud she would be that we made it. If I had stayed and chosen to believe the hateful things spewed at me back then, I wouldn't be living my passion. I wouldn't be three years strong in a business that is not just a business, but a movement to teach and support a healthier lifestyle. That thought both saddens me and strengthens my resolve to be the difference that I needed then and still do—the difference that SO MANY need when faced with taking control of their health.

I like to think that God and my mom are up there smiling at the warrior I've become. While it's easier to remember this on some days than others, I know in my heart that I am living my purpose. And I'm not done yet. Not by a long shot.

Take the Risk

Carrie Williams

Carrie Williams, CPA and owner of Running Valley Financial, is great at crunching numbers, but it's not a love for numbers that drives her work; it's a love for people. Whether she's helping hard working people get the most from each dollar they earn through financial coaching or empowering small business owners to run profitable businesses and reduce taxes, Carrie seeks to leave a positive imprint on the lives of others.

After a lengthy career in corporate America, Carrie was ready for a change and felt a strong pull to make a greater impact. Then the pandemic hit. The desire to have more flexibility in her schedule, coupled with the fact that the pandemic was turning many families' financial situations upside down, made it the right time to start her financial business, where she could make a positive impact for others immediately.

Carrie's individual clients are often people who are earning good money but can't seem to make the progress they would like toward reducing their debt or increasing their savings. Her business clients are those who desire to create generational wealth for their families. Her wrap-around financial services include tax preparation for individuals and small businesses.

When Carrie is not helping people maximize their financial resources, she loves to volunteer with United Way Suncoast through their Financial Stability initiatives. Carrie also enjoys traveling, the outdoors, and supporting her children's sports with her husband by her side.

———

Most would never see a quiet, reserved, rule-following girl from a small town in North Dakota as a gambler—especially not an accountant. It just doesn't seem like it would be in the cards. But I'm here to tell you that life's too short to play it safe and play it small.

Here's how I know.

I've always had a competitive spirit with a streak of determination. Maybe it's the luck of the draw from my heritage: a combination of Scandinavian (resilient), and Scottish (stubborn). Early on, I became laser-focused on success. As a result, I was a high achiever in academics, but I was still playing the game conservatively.

The first gamble presented itself in my fourth year of college where I applied for internships and hit the jackpot by getting accepted to one—in Florida. Looking back, I am proud of myself for making that bold decision to double down. Somehow my gut was telling me I needed to do it. So, I went all in and headed south, arriving on the doorstep of a soon-to-be coworker who offered to rent out a room to me. I didn't know anyone in the state.

At that point in my life, I was ready to sit at a new table and start a new game. It was a blank slate to create the future I wanted, and I remember being more excited than afraid.

I had played my cards right, and that bold move upped the ante for me. After I finished school, I was offered a full-time position with that same company. To sweeten the deal, I had met someone in Florida who would end up being my future husband, so the decision was an easy one. I moved to Tampa permanently. To say it was a culture shock coming from a tiny town of 1,000 people would be an understatement. But I soaked everything in as a learning experience, and it was invigorating to broaden my horizons.

My second significant gamble was when I applied for my first promotion. It was an accounting supervisor position in a male-dominated manufacturing area of the business. I was about 24 years old, sweet, quiet, and reserved. This job would take me out of the comforts of the corporate office and place me in a less-refined environment. When an old-timer at the office heard that I was applying for the position, he scoffed, "You can't do that job." It's amazing what words will do. I knew then that I was one of those people who uses those kinds of words as motivation when the chips are down. From there, I created a mindset of, "Watch me. I'll do it, and do it better than anyone else before me." Relying on my grit, tenacity, and determination, I set out to prove the doubters wrong.

And it worked. I was slaying, and I was running the table.

The next few years took me through the highs and lows of life's milestones. The company became a constant in my life, and I felt that I would retire there. I got married (yes, to the one I had met on my internship), had two beautiful children, had two miscarriages, and got divorced. After I had my first child, I was so devoted to work that I took the minimum maternity leave to come back to work as soon as possible. I was self-driven and determined to rise to the top in a male-dominated environment. I remember pumping breastmilk in the office bathroom (before offices having dedicated rooms for that was a thing).

Being a mom and balancing a demanding career is not easy, and there is no balance. But I kept doing what I thought I was supposed to do: graduate from college, get a good job with a big, stable company, and remain there for the rest of my career. I had checked all those boxes. But nobody tells you what to do then. There is no playbook for life.

With the kids in daycare, my then-husband traveling for work, and me at the office (before working from home was a thing), I was stretched too thin. But I was successful, receiving a promotion every few years. I established myself as a go-to person to get results. Career-wise, I held all the aces. I was rewarded for being driven, dedicated, and focused. Meanwhile, my marriage was the equivalent of a busted flush because we didn't communicate. At one point, we contemplated a decision to cash in my chips and stay home with the kids. We could have afforded it, but I didn't want to. And the mom guilt rushed in because I felt like I was choosing my career over raising my kids, and people were judging me for it. But I felt that I was wired to work, and I was good at it.

I believe that everything happens for a reason. When we ultimately got divorced, I still had my source of income, so I was able to make the decision to walk away. However, I had mom guilt again, worrying about what was best for the kids.

It was a gamble because I didn't know how it was going to turn out. But it was a risk worth taking to have a happier life.

I was naïve in thinking I had found the perfect career with a great company, and it would last forever. Nobody told me that the game changes over time, whether it's mergers or changes in leadership. Also, beliefs in company loyalty completely shifted during that time. When I graduated, the "ideal" path was to get a good job with a good company, remain loyal, and retire from there. But somewhere down the line, the deck became stacked against the people who followed that path. The new corporate leadership mentality was that they favor employees who move around and experience different ways of doing things.

To stay with one company meant you had bet all your chips on one hand.

As I matured and was able to start looking at my career through a different lens, I came to realize that my skills and experience were no longer valued. I was an "old-timer" at the age of 44 because I already had a 20-year career with the company. I started to get turned down for promotions and other opportunities.

All bets were off.

When you're in the middle of something, you can't truly see what is happening until you get to the other side and can reflect via a bird's eye view. What I didn't realize was that my quality of life was deteriorating and my stress was increasing alongside my unhappiness. I would come home frustrated and transfer that frustration to my family. The game was no longer fun to play.

Looking back, I realize that many instances occurred where clearly God was trying to show me that this was not for me anymore. But I refused to see it, telling myself that I should be fortunate to have the hand I was dealt.

It took a pandemic and some egregious events for me to call a spade a spade and realize that I needed to make a change. I was determined to go out on my own terms and create the future that I was meant to live. My competitive drive became the ace up my sleeve.

My biggest gamble taken to date has been deciding to leave the security of my corporate career that was no longer serving me and start my own financial company. It's been the greatest risk but has had the biggest rewards. I no longer dread the upcoming workweek. I have flexibility beyond measure, where I can work from home, dictate my own schedule, and be there for my family. My stress level has decreased immensely, and I am now able to enjoy life and all that it brings with my new husband by my side.

I never thought I would become an entrepreneur, but I feel like I've hit the jackpot once again. I am challenged daily by figuring out the intricacies of running a business and finding ways to scale and increase profits. And I have the extremely fulfilling opportunity to help everyday people make the most of their hard-earned money and coach them on how to run profitable businesses that can create generational wealth. If I had never taken the risk, I would never have experienced the reward, and I would not have been able to make this level of impact for others.

As an accountant, I've learned the art of taking calculated risks. When deciding whether to take a leap, think about what is the worst outcome that can happen. There is rarely a decision where you can't change course or go a different path if something doesn't work out. Just don't bet more than you can afford to lose.

So take the risk, don't play small, and start slaying!

Life's Echoes Unfiltered

Dr. Maram Bishawi

Dedicated to my father, who taught me resilience, my mother, who taught me how to love, my brother Muath, who always motivated me academically, my brother Mohammad, who always grounds me, my sister Mira, who gave me a lifetime best friend, and my youngest brother Mumen, who makes me feel whole.

Dr. Maram Bishawi is a tenacious and resilient soul, driven by an adventurous spirit and an unending thirst for knowledge. She takes great pride in her Arab-American heritage, which has been a significant source of inspiration throughout her life.

With unwavering determination, Maram overcame numerous challenges, forging a path to become the first female in her family to pursue advanced studies and achieve her dream of becoming a physician. Today, she practices emergency medicine with unwavering passion and also serves as one of the trauma doctors for the Lightning hockey team, a role she holds dear.

Beyond the field of medicine, her world revolves around her close-knit family and cherished friends. She treasures every moment shared with them. As a mentor to many young women, she ignites the flames of ambition, guiding them toward their aspirations. An avid lover of an active, outdoorsy lifestyle, she thrives in the open air. Her creative spirit finds expression in activities such as baking, traveling, everything fitness, and various artistic pursuits. Music resonates with her soul, harmonizing with her overarching purpose in life: to serve and assist others. Together, these aspects weave the intricate tapestry of her unique and remarkable life.

———

Born and raised in the lively city of Amman, Jordan, I often found myself labeled as a "rebel" by many, yet I preferred to see myself as an intrepid explorer. Even before the age of 11, I embarked on solitary urban expeditions armed with my trusty fanny pack stocked with snacks and a magnifying glass, as I delved into my quest for new adventures. My spirit exuded a tomboyish enthusiasm, making it nearly impossible for me to remain still—I was perpetually drawn to the allure of new adventures. My curiosity often led me into situations that earned me the playful moniker "mother-in-law" by my teachers at my private school... let's just say that wasn't a compliment! What truly enamored me, however, was the profound richness and beauty of my culture. Despite my fortunate birth into a well-educated and refined family, I constantly eluded the traditional expectations imposed upon women. It was almost as though I had misplaced my personal guidebook on how to be the "perfect Arab daughter."

In the summer of 2000, I was on the cusp of turning 12 when my family made the life-changing move to the United States, more specifically, New York. Boarding a plane for this adventure felt effortless; I had been assured that it was the very land where "the Smurfs" resided. My childhood obsession was about to merge with reality, as I was about to encounter what seemed like the real-life Smurfs. My parents held steadfast to the belief in providing us with boundless opportunities. Both sets of my grandparents had previously migrated from Palestine to Jordan, and it was now my father's turn to ensure that his children had access to endless opportunities, particularly in education. He understood that the trajectory of our lives would have been significantly different had we remained in Jordan. His decision to uproot our familiar lives for the challenges of an unfamiliar one is an act I deeply admire.

I am the second of five children, the eldest daughter in the family. Looking back, I'd like to believe I was an easy child to raise, though I'm increasingly convinced that I gave my parents a run for their money. I have a vivid memory of my father sitting down with my older brother and me, imparting a profound message about the transformative potential of this move. He emphasized that we could become anything we aspired to be but that it would require hard work. He warned us about the challenges we'd encounter, but in our eyes, the allure of the "land of opportunity" overshadowed any apprehension. With a 13-year-old boy and an 11-year-old girl enthusiastically in agreement, he handed us an Arabic-English dictionary as our guide for charting our path forward.

The language barrier worked to my advantage in some ways, especially since the 9/11 attacks occurred just a couple of months after our arrival. At that time, I only knew a few words of English, so any potential discrimination I might have faced as an Arab-

American went largely unnoticed, as I genuinely couldn't understand much of what was said to me. My journey to learning English was made possible by Nickelodeon's *Rugrats* and the Junie B. Jones books. A short episode would easily take me hours as I paused for English subtitles and translated them into Arabic. My dictionary was well-loved and held together by wads of tape. I felt ecstatic at the end of each episode when I could understand the themes of the Rugrat babies. Although mastering the English language took some time, I excelled in my academic pursuits.

One of the primary reasons my parents favored raising their children in the United States was the abundant educational opportunities it promised. Given my strong aptitude for math and the sciences, I gained admission to a bridge program, enabling me to commence my college studies at the tender age of 16. Observing my passion for science, my parents encouraged me to pursue a career in the field and eventually steered me toward becoming a pharmacist. This choice made sense, given the appealing aspects of the profession: favorable work hours, a six-year path to a doctorate, a lucrative income, and a familial connection as my father's closest friend happened to be a pharmacist in Jordan. The decision was a clear one. I, too, was a meticulous planner, envisioning a future where I would attain a doctorate in pharmacy, be happily married, and have two or three children by the age of 22. This not only satisfied my sense of organization but would bring immense pride to my family.

Unbeknownst to my parents, my life's trajectory was about to take a dramatic turn as I began to dream of venturing far from home to pursue an independent college experience, a dream uncommon for girls with my background. Following my two-year associate degree, my parents presented me with various options for nearby colleges that would allow me to live at home and commute to school. Out of all these choices, I applied to just one institution: Rutgers University in New Jersey, renowned as one of the top pharmacy schools at the time. My elation knew no bounds when I received acceptance into their cell biology and neuroscience program.

I held this exciting news close to my heart, applying for an early summer program without disclosing a word of it to my parents. I deliberately chose to reveal my plans only two weeks before the program's commencement, knowing that, at that point, their ability to deter me was limited. No other colleges had been considered, and my acceptance was already secured. To them, I was ardently pursuing my "pharmacy dreams," although my enthusiasm for this career had waned after a summer working as a pharmacy tech, a change of heart I never shared with them.

My parents reluctantly acquiesced to my decision. However, I soon discovered that campus housing was significantly more expensive, which led me to choose a somewhat dubious apartment in New Brunswick, shared with three roommates. An intriguing twist was that my roommates wouldn't arrive until the fall, granting me a couple of solitary months. But it didn't take long for misfortune to knock on my door in the form of a burglary that left me with a broken lock, as my landlord mysteriously vanished. This was a detail I had concealed from my parents initially, fearing they might insist I return home. Thus, I spent the next month clutching a kitchen knife beneath my pillow, all the while consumed by anxiety.

Eventually, my parents discovered that my major wasn't pharmacy but neuroscience, a revelation that greatly disconcerted them as they couldn't fathom what I'd do with it. Truth be told, I was unsure myself. It wasn't until I encountered a sign—quite literally, a sign in the school cafeteria—that essentially asked, "Do you love science but don't know what to do?" Alongside it were flyers for a program in Scranton, Pa., designed to help explore one's options. It was as if the universe was speaking directly to me, and I knew what I had to do. I applied to and was accepted into a program in Scranton, where I pursued a master's in biomedical sciences. Having been raised in the capital city of Jordan and spending time near New York City, I knew nothing about rural America. It was a surreal experience, and in the midst of this quiet environment, I forged friendships that would endure a lifetime.

One serendipitous day, I mistakenly wandered into a meeting meant for current medical students interested in emergency medicine (ER), instead of the planned informative PhD gathering I was signed up for. In my heels and suit, I felt out of place, but I decided to stay to avoid seeming impolite, sitting discreetly at the back, thinking I was overdressed. After the lecture, an older Irish physician, Dr. O'Brien noticed my presence and remarked that I didn't belong there—an assertion I readily agreed with. A conversation ensued, and he saw something in me that I couldn't quite comprehend. He wholeheartedly believed I was meant to be a physician, particularly an ER physician. After some initial resistance, I agreed to shadow him in the ER, a specialty that I wholeheartedly fell in love with. The blend of excitement, adrenaline, variety, and constant movement ignited a passion within me, making me want to be just like Dr. O'Brien. However, the path to becoming a doctor, from prerequisite classes to MCATs to volunteer work, was long and arduous. I briefly strayed from this dream, becoming an adjunct professor at a college while preparing for medical school with whatever precious time I could spare between my three jobs.

My life was nearly extinguished one fateful night when I decided to surprise my parents with a drive to New York. It was a snowy evening, and as I navigated the winding hills of Pennsylvania, fate took a perilous turn. An 18-wheeler sideswiped my car, causing it to careen off the side of a cliff, almost swallowed by a heavy snowdrift. Though I never lost consciousness, I lay there, wide awake, for nearly an hour, in a state I now recognize as shock. Later, I would learn that my spine and ribcage were shattered. It's moments like these that solidify my faith: a man seemingly materialized out of thin air, but how did he even know there was a car down there? This question will linger with me for the rest of my days. He revealed only his name and mentioned he worked for a nearby florist before vanishing into thin air just as the ambulance arrived.

That night, in the hospital, a neurosurgeon delivered a grim prognosis. The good news was that I was alive, but the bad news was that I'd be confined to a wheelchair for the remainder of my life. I had lost all sensation in my legs, and my spine was still in shock. As a once-active young woman, this felt like a death sentence. For the next 24 hours, nobody knew for certain, as I remained in the ICU under constant monitoring. Amidst hallucinations of elephants induced by Morphine and the incessant blaring of alarms, I suddenly felt my nurse poking my feet, and I screamed. It was my favorite pain, as I knew I had regained sensation, and I wasn't truly paralyzed.

In the following months, I embarked on a relentless quest to find the man who had saved me, and to express my gratitude for giving me a second chance at life. I called every florist in the area in an attempt to track him down, as I remembered he was a local. My search proved fruitless, but it only strengthened my belief that he was destined to save me and grant me the opportunity to start anew. To literally learn how to walk again. If he ever happens to read this, I hope he realizes what a precious life he spared and how many lives I, in turn, have saved since.

Those months in recovery were an arduous journey. My strong-willed nature led me to reject surgery, and instead, I relied on sheer determination to regain my ability to walk. Through the practice of yoga and meditation, I endeavored to overcome the challenges, even when conventional physical therapy was deemed too risky due to my instability. As I gazed at the bottle of pain pills they had prescribed, I confronted a pivotal moment. I made the conscious choice to discard them, watching as they dissolved slowly, disappearing into the toilet. This marked a turning point, for those pills were proficient at numbing not only physical pain but also the emotional turmoil that I found even more daunting.

Little did I realize that this accident, which had initially brought me to the brink of despair, would later emerge as the most transformative event in my life. It compelled me to elevate and take my commitment to pursuing a career in medicine seriously. My guiding motto became crystal clear: never take away hope. I pressed forward with unwavering perseverance.

At the age of 27, unmarried and without children, I became an ER physician, practicing and learning medicine in the high-pressure environment of a level-one trauma center. Every dream I had ever harbored materialized into reality. It was not merely a personal triumph but a victory for my entire family. Since then, I have lived my life unfiltered, breaking through barriers I once thought impossible. That snowy canyon night, I believe, echoed my life's purpose: to serve, to assist others, and to save lives. Although my journey may not have followed a predictable trajectory, it was undoubtedly steered by destiny.

Trusting & Believing in Me

Parita Patel

My name is Parita Patel and I run a health insurance agency in Tampa, Fla. My career in this industry began in 2021, and it has skyrocketed in the last few years. The private insurance space is unique and helps individuals, business owners, and families save thousands of dollars each year in healthcare expenses. I have one of the top teams in the country with over 45+ agents dedicated to helping others.

My biggest passions in life are leadership and personal development, and I am striving to become the absolute elite and best version of myself. The true measure of leadership is the ability to inspire others, and through leading by example, I know I can show people how possible it is to achieve your wildest goals and desires if you just work hard enough for it.

My dream for the future is to speak in front of thousands of students to help them do the same. I aspire to be a mom and wife and recognize that without a family, one will never truly feel fulfilled and challenged.

―――

After only 33 years of living, I feel like I have already lived multiple lives. Each chapter has a story, and every story has contributed to my journey of love and loss, growth and challenge, pain and learning.

The first time I "woke up" was the day after my 25th birthday. I remember looking around me, piecing together the night before, and realizing that this was not a life I was happy living. My whole life, I was given the message to go to school and get good grades, get a job that pays me well, and find a man to settle down with. This was the meaning of life.

So, at the point of my 25th birthday, I'd accomplished the first two. But I remember waking up that morning wondering why I was living for the weekends and miserable outside of them. I was in a constant state of feeling empty and uninspired. I was a zombie going through the motions. It felt as though my life was living "for" me, rather than me living my life.

I woke up that morning and asked myself, *is this what it has all been for*? Just then, I knew that it was time to make a change.

As a first-generation Indian woman in America, my parents instilled an intense work ethic in me. If I did anything, I did it to an extreme... almost to a fault. Once I surpassed all expectations and successfully achieved all challenges placed before me, it was always a question of "what's next." There was never any stopping to celebrate or appreciate what I *had* achieved.

I always dreamt of achieving greatness—but didn't know what that meant. What I did know was that it was not going to happen where I was: Corporate America. This is where the soul goes to die, where all inspiration ceases. Here I was, completing a 40-hour-a-week job in half the time... so was *that* my big accomplishment?

My search for more began that morning after my birthday. It took all the strength and courage I had to leave it all behind and find something that would make me feel alive again. After having spent two years each in Minnesota and Texas, I moved back to Florida in 2015. And so began the next story, which was a phase of love and challenge.

As I was approaching my 30s, the pressure of settling down and finding someone to share my life with was growing— particularly from having grown up in an Indian household. I remember when my father said to me, "Maybe your expectations or standards are just too high." I didn't realize at the time how this would impact my next decision.

I met someone, and, like many women, let the idea of him being "the one" be front-and-center. I didn't let red flags or negative experiences deter me from that path. I opened my heart to love and simultaneously opened my mind to an entrepreneurial path because I knew I had to change my career. I decided to search based on my passions and stumbled on a boutique fitness studio with a high-tech workout. This changed my life for the next three years. I was a personal trainer at first, but I started developing the owner's business, and he quickly promoted me to be his chief operating officer.

I grew this business and wore all the hats: sales, marketing through social media, hiring, training, operations, and more. As I grew the business, I grew personally. The newly-gifted ring on my finger signified that the next phase of life was about to commence. My career thrived. We grew from one to six studios across the United States, but unfortunately, they had to shut down with the pandemic.

The career that I had been spending 80 hours a week building was now lost. But on the other hand, the relationship I had been working so hard on was flourishing now that we were married... at least, this is what's supposed to happen, right?

I have a huge capacity for love and tend to only see the good in people. This has always been a double-edged sword for me. I forgive them for misdoings and make excuses for their behavior. These are all the things that make me who I am—but they're also the root causes of the pain I continue to experience. I love hard, and because my heart is so big, I hurt deeply too.

My husband was a good man, raised by a good family, and we aligned in many ways. But it never felt like he tried to know ME. When the pandemic hit, every relationship had to have been hit too. Being forced to be with someone 24/7 was definitely a challenge for me. Yet I was the one who thought that once I earned the title of "wife," maybe then I would matter more and be treated better by my husband. I asked him one day if he ever wakes up and thinks to himself, "How can I make my wife smile today?" His response: "You have an unrealistic view and expectation of what marriage is."

By this point, he had hurt me enough times that I had already fallen out of love with him, but I would continue to work at it because of my culture. I was taught that to marry meant to enter a life with someone forever.

It was time to re-enter the workforce. The fitness industry was all but destroyed, and I didn't have the means to build something of my own yet, so my goal was to make enough money that I could support myself in every way. I did not want to ask my husband for money because when he would say "no," even for the littlest of things, it stung; a girl can only take so much rejection. The one thing I did know is that I have always been a career-oriented woman, and I believed in the power of hard work. Within 24 hours of updating my resume on Indeed.com, I received multiple interview requests, including one from an insurance agency.

Little did I know that this opportunity would change my life forever.

When I started, I was already broken. How could I not be after losing my career and living in a loveless marriage? I desperately needed a win to help me start rebuilding my confidence. After a few weeks, I realized I had a knack for it. Sales was all about talking to people, and that had always been a strong suit of mine. I finally could afford a therapist—and thank God, because my personal life was getting worse. I learned what the term "gaslighting" meant, and that it had been happening to me for the past seven years. We tried therapy together, where he blamed me for being in this position now and insisted that nothing was his fault. He attempted for two weeks to rebuild with me and then gave up.

I had a conversation with his mom, and she said, "What do you think a man's job is in a marriage? It's to provide, which my son has generously done all these years. It is not to provide emotional support." After hearing that, I knew it could never work, because clearly this mindset was ingrained in him from birth.

They tell you divorce is hard, but it's impossible to describe. I read an article that said, "Divorce is equivalent to the death of a loved one," and I agree. The pain is heavy and lasts longer than anything. It leaves a mark on you that will resurface when you least expect it. While this was happening, my career took a turn... the kind that most people dream of. Everything happens for a reason, right?

I poured myself into my job, and through my efforts on social media building trusted relationships, I changed the face of the industry forever. In year one, I went from having $1,500 to my name to making six figures. In year two, I became the number one insurance agent and first female in the history of the company to hold the title. Today I have my own agency with a team of 45+ agents. If I were still married, none of this would have been possible. I know now that my ex had wanted a trophy wife at home — someone to cater to him, who wouldn't dare earn more than he did. If I were still with him, I would not be who I am today: a strong female who is out-earning and out-achieving everyone in a male-dominated industry, and setting records that are miles ahead of the previous achievers. The current story I am in now is the one that I am meant to write. Every experience I've had has prepared me for the life I am living today. My mission is clear: to empower others, identify the strengths they have within, and challenge them to live the life they had always wanted.

You do not need someone else. You only need to trust and believe in yourself.

Onward and Upward

Nicole Carver

Nicole Carver is a lifestyle manager and CEO of Carver Concierge, a boutique personal concierge and lifestyle management agency. She's also a mom of three, a military spouse, and an active community member. For over ten years, Carver Concierge has provided high-touch, skilled luxury lifestyle management and personal assistance services to help busy and discerning people focus on the things that bring them joy or make them money.

With teams in Tampa, Fla., and Nashville, Tenn., Carver's personable concierge, along with their expansive network of vetted partner professionals, offer clientele geographically unlimited virtual services and boots on the ground support—everything busy professionals need to enhance their lifestyles and get back their time. Nicole and her team not only want to meet clients' needs but exceed their expectations with every service they provide.

———

As the plane takes off from Tampa airport, I think about how many miles I've flown over the years before I touched down in the place I've landed as a woman. Today, I can say I travel frequently, but my journeys really didn't take place until later in life. Ahead of that though, my road was well traveled, most certainly through different states of mind. The one place that would always be home, no matter how large or small, was with my family.

I was born in a small town in Vermont. The farthest I would travel would be with my dad, in the summers, as he worked his routes across the country as a long haul trucker. There were no big city experiences on those treks, rather stops in other small towns across America for the few weeks I'd go each year. My brother and I would alternate. In retrospect, I think it was a means to give my mom a much needed break. While Dad traveled, she steadily worked as a hairdresser, balancing business and children as gracefully as one could. To this day, at over 80 years young, my mom is still making each day count taking care of her clients. Something I'd later appreciate more than I did at the time.

On days Mom was working in the shop, we'd stay with my grandmother. She lived in New Hampshire... and that may seem like a far distance to be a state away, but she was closer than your nearest market. Our small town in Vermont bordered New Hampshire, so within five minutes of the bus dropping us off we'd be at her home a state away. We were always a close family that looked out for one another, and together I watched the women I admired handle all the logistics that made our life run smoothly and happily.

When I say a "small town," please understand that I mean that my high school graduating class still debates on whether there were 30 or 40 of us in total. My brother, God rest his soul, and I were five years apart in age and consistently graced the same hallways no matter how far the age gap. For most of the kids in our town, you had a few options after you finished school, and those were to be a teacher, be in the military, or find a local business to work with.

I chose the latter and began working straight out of school. I took a job with a national hockey equipment company. I remember being so proud to work for the president and the vice president. Until the first thing they did was ask me to make coffee, and I was just as indignant as I would be now about it.

I made them the worst pot of coffee they ever had and was told "Nicole, don't ever make my coffee again." Luckily, my administrative and organizational skills were far more superior than my barista skills.

In March of 1992, I married my high school sweetheart, and we began planning for the perfect future. I joined Blue Cross and Blue Shield for almost a decade. I loved the organizational elements and helping people. It's always been my passion to solve problems and find ways to efficiently get things done. I mean, no one ever thanks you for processing their insurance claims, but I knew I'd made people's lives easier, and that meant so much to me.

Then one night, my life changed directions. I received a call that my husband had been killed in a snowmobiling accident, only 9 months after we said "I do." I wish I could recall the cold numbness I felt becoming a widow at 25, but it's still lost on me. Following the pain and sadness, life blessed me with two beautiful sons, Kyle and Trace, and another marriage, a divorce, and many life lessons.

I eventually landed a job with the State of Vermont working as an executive level assistant. It was exciting to be front and center working for commissioners, secretaries of state, and the like. I genuinely enjoyed seeing behind the scenes of the process of our government and felt empowered to serve the state and our communities. I thrived under pressure with my logistical loving heart fluttering.

Another day would come and change the path of my journey. As a single mom with two young sons, I found myself in the aisles of Walmart one afternoon. As a typical small town New England raised girl, the checkout lines are meant for chatter. I struck up a conversation with a nice-looking man as he processed his small, bachelor-looking grocery order.

I left the store, and he followed me down the mall corridor and asked me if I'd like to go to lunch with him sometime. I said "Well maybe, if you mean dinner," and handed him my business card, and he handed me his. It may sound vain, but I was shocked that he didn't reach out after nearly five days had passed.

I took the risk of being bold, and sent an email that said, "Did you lose my card or just your interest?"

His reply let me know that he hadn't lost either. My face was bright red when I checked my spam folder to see our connection was not missed. We did have that dinner, and the journey that has unfolded since has been epic.

Drew was an Army officer living in Vermont at the time because he was teaching ROTC at Norwich University and Dartmouth College, after returning from a deployment. We went on dates for the months to come before he received orders to move to Kansas for his next phase of military training as our love deepened, and we made it work from a distance until finally he flew home on Columbus Day in 2007 and we married.

By that December, we got news he'd be stationed in Germany. So we packed up our separate homes and the boys, and I flew to

Germany with him to begin our lives for the first time as a family. It would be the first time we'd live under one roof. My boys were now 6 and 12, and they were so excited to go on an adventure across the world, and what an adventure it was.

For me, this small-town girl from a little part of Vermont, it was pure magic. We traveled, took in the culture, and lived on the base. We'd learned a bit of the language, and the boys adjusted so well. I had expected to easily find a job on base, but I quickly found that those opportunities were limited. I fell under the wing of an amazing woman, a military spouse, who allowed me an opportunity to create a sustainable program for incoming spouses, and in 2008, we learned that I was about to be a mother again. Our family became a party of five in 2009 when we welcomed our daughter Sophia.

We'd spend almost five years in Germany before we received orders to return to the United States to settle in Tampa. I was ready to start a new chapter in my career. I spent most of my time in Germany on family logistics or volunteering. Building a career around my kids was still so important to me, especially without family nearby and with my husband gone so often. I needed something to fill my bucket that allowed me family flexibility.

What started out as a plan to provide administrative support for busy entrepreneurs quickly changed direction after being asked many times over if I had time to wait for the plumber or pick up the dry cleaning. I saw the gap that almost all busy executives were experiencing in the day-to-day logistics. I wanted to fill that need to get all the other things off their to-do list aside from working hard and doing what gave them joy. I knew there must be a need for someone to call the insurance company, handle scheduling the maintenance folks, take the dog to the vet and so forth. I wanted to create a business that helped solve for those needs.

As someone who always loved efficiency and problem solving, creating Carver Concierge was a delight. I hired a couple other military spouses who were looking for extra work. We realized how many people, like us, struggle to get all the things on the list done. Having a team to ease that burden gives space for a more peaceful life. The business took off. We've now expanded operations into the Nashville market as well, specifically in Franklin and Brentwood, Tenn.

Most days between projects in flight, or literally in flight myself between two cities, I am so proud of the journey I've been on. What I've learned most about where I've landed as a woman is to expect the unexpected. It's critical to plan for the joy, and move past the sorrow. A life well lived is one where you take the leap, are bold, and know you'll always catch yourself if you fall. Home will always be where your heart is, no matter how that changes over time, so always make room for others to live in it.

New Beginnings

Genesis Krick

Genesis Hey Krick, M.A., CLC, is a thrill seeker, an adventurous spirit, and an inspirational powerhouse. She is a mom of four, an executive business coach, and a high-performance strategist. She works with high-profile women who are ready to serve their clients in a higher capacity while still maintaining balance and stability within their personal and professional lives. She is the founder and CEO of Dream Ignite Build which provides coaching, community, and connection to established business owners and individuals who are ready to scale and make big shifts to create new opportunities and pursue higher levels of success. She has written and collaborated on five books, with her most popular being *Unleash Your Potential*. She has spoken to hundreds of organizations, sharing her message and inspiring individuals across the world by giving hope that a new beginning is always possible. Genesis has over 10 years of experience working with entrepreneurs and high-level executives. When she isn't working with clients you will find Genesis writing her next book, going for a run, or spending time with her kiddos drinking coffee and eating cake pops!

———

Adventure and risk-taking have always been an integral part of my life, with each season bringing the excitement and thrill of the great unknown. Growing up on 13 acres of land helped to solidify that mindset of having no fear; throughout my childhood, I'd climb to the treetops, walk alone in the dark woods, and run around in thunderstorms.

Yet even as a young child, I knew there was so much more out there to explore.

Fast-forward 20 years and you'd find me on a rooftop in downtown Chicago, sipping a glass of pinot grigio. After living in the city for eight years, I realized I had outgrown my living situation and felt as though I needed to make a dramatic move. That move would mean my life would be forever changed.

I was single with no kids. I'd just graduated from a master's program and was turning 27. I figured there was no better time to leave. Chicago was an amazing city, and living downtown was an absolute dream in many ways. Still, if I left, I would be leaving everything I had ever known behind.

Though I had moved to Chicago from a small town, I was still in Illinois, an hour and a half from where I grew up, and I couldn't be more comfortable continuing to do the same things and going through the progressions. I was definitely at a crossroads. I would be walking away from a great job that I loved, a beautiful condo on Michigan Avenue that I was planning to purchase from my grandparents, and all the amazing relationships that I'd built over the years.

I knew that starting over somewhere else would be hard, but there was something inside of me that just knew if I didn't, I would wonder "what if" forever.

From the time I was young, I had a burning desire to move to L.A. There was something innately inside of me that was calling me to be there. I had always heard that L.A. was the land of opportunity and that if you wanted to make it big, that was the place to go. Although I believed in fully pursuing this incredible move, I felt deeply that there was something else outside of the opportunity that was drawing me there. I guess it was a sense that that could be my destiny.

As I sipped my wine and looked out at the skyline, all the magnificent oranges, reds, and pink hues had an indescribable glow that embodied the moment. As I stared intently at the sky, I got a call from a girlfriend who had previously lived in L.A. but had since moved back to Colorado. "Girl, I decided to move back to L.A.!" she exclaimed. "Would you consider coming with me and being my roommate?"

There are moments in life when you realize that God is at work, and you know that there is no possible way that whatever is happening is just coincidence. This was one of those moments. I was ecstatic. I told her how I was feeling, and that change was calling my name loudly. She asked, "What are you waiting for!?"

I was silent for what seemed like an eternity. I knew that saying goodbye to everything I knew would be really hard. But then I thought back to all of the things that had led me there, and I realized it all was meant for this moment. "Let's do it!" I yelled.

We were ecstatic and started making plans right away.

Four weeks later, my mom and I were headed to L.A. Driving out west with my mom is one of my fondest memories, and we took full advantage of the experiences along the way—we drove through ghost towns, hit museums, and fully embraced the beautiful scenery!

As we drew nearer to L.A., the excitement was building. Each mile closer was one mile that I had never gone before. And then we saw the sign: *Welcome to Fabulous Los Angeles, California.*

I knew at that moment that I was exactly where I was meant to be.

We pulled into our gorgeous gated community in the heart of L.A. across the street from The Grove. Once we were settled, I looked around and felt a great sense of peace knowing that I was listening to the call on my heart. This was it... I was *here*. My sweet mom stayed for about a week and then flew back. I wept when she left because, regardless of how excited I was about being there, I would miss her (and all my loved ones) so much!

Immediately I started getting plugged in. I met amazing people within my community, applied for new jobs, and became immersed in L.A. culture. It was such a fun time! I knew I needed to get back into my workout routine, so I found some classes to try at a community gym. The gorgeous facility was decked out in white and gold and featured a stunning fitness room.

After I arrived, I stretched and chatted with a few others in the class. Within a few minutes, a beautiful, buff man with a dark complexion walked in. The connection was instant, and I knew right away that I had to talk to him. We had a great workout. Afterward, I thought I'd ask him a few questions and our chat turned into a meaningful conversation, then a date. We went out again and again, and pretty soon I realized that this was the person I wanted to spend my life with.

Within a few months, I moved out of the house I'd been sharing with my friend and into his small studio apartment. Two people living in the tiniest space you can imagine was a true testament of love! Life was simple. We didn't have much money, but we thought we could make it work. I had always wanted to have a family and get married, but he had been married previously and wasn't sure if he would want to again. Days turned into months, and the time passed quickly. Nothing was changing, and I felt as though we would be in this continuous downward spiral forever! I couldn't allow myself to continue in this situation. I wanted to be with someone who was fully committed to me and the life we had together.

What I realized after countless conversations and frustrating setbacks was that what I thought was meant for forever turned into something quite different. I recognized that I was not going to change someone else's mindset, goals, or future projections. How I saw life was not necessarily how someone else viewed life. I recognized that love alone was not enough to make a relationship work.

After countless attempts to bring things back together, I moved out.

Moving out and moving on was painful, especially because it felt like I'd realized a dream that couldn't be achieved. I was desperate to find something that gave me comfort, but I wasn't ready to give up on L.A.—after all, I'd gone there for a reason, and it certainly wasn't to go right back to Illinois! After quickly scouring the area, I found a cute apartment in walking distance of almost everything I needed. Starting over would be hard, but I knew I could make things work by keeping the mindset of taking one day at a time.

After a few weeks, I really started getting settled in and decided I would start going out with friends to fully explore the new area. As I got ready to head out, I couldn't help but feel that there was something not quite right. I didn't feel well and was absolutely exhausted. I decided to hang back and take a little rest. I have never been a napper, so for me to feel I needed to lie down was wild. I woke up a few hours later still tired. I couldn't help but think there was something seriously wrong.

Then, I realized it was that time of the month, so I figured that must be why. But after several days, I still didn't feel well. I grabbed a pregnancy test to calm my nerves. I took the test and set it on the bathroom sink, knowing full well that it would be negative. I went to the kitchen to start making dinner. As I walked back into the bathroom to confirm what I already knew, I gasped and took a step back. Panic set in.

The test showed I *was* pregnant!

Oh no! I thought. *There must be a mistake!*

I went back to the store and bought three more tests (as if the more I bought, the more likely it would be that one would be negative). After four positive tests, I called my mom and shared the news. She was silent on the other end of the phone and then finally said, "Genesis, come home." Within a week she was there helping me pack up my things. Two years of L.A. glamor and opportunity all changed within a second. I would be heading back to Illinois with my mom, and I was devastated. I would be leaving behind everything that I had created in this new life.

How could this be happening to me? I wasn't married, and I didn't want to go back to a small town where there was nothing for me.

On the way home I felt just about every emotion possible, from sadness to anger, guilt, and anxiety. The great unknown had struck again, and here I was headed back to a small town to start over at the age of 29.

How could I face the people that have known me my whole life? How could I disappoint so many? I didn't want this to be my story.

I felt sick the whole way home. I was almost to the point of dry heaving and had chills. Just when I thought it couldn't get much worse, we pulled into the small town of Dixon, and I saw a sign with a quote by Ronald Reagan, "A Great Place to Come Home to." That was true—it *was* a great place to come home to, even under difficult circumstances.

It took a few days to unload my stuff and for me to process what just happened. My whole life had been taken out from under me in a matter of days, and the timeline I had planned on no longer existed. I sat at home in the room that I grew up in and looked around. The beautiful blue room with clouds around the border, looking as if I was outside on a beautiful day, was very calming. Days passed, and with each one I was awoken by a beautiful orchestra of birds and nature sounds. As sad as I was, I felt so much peace and contentment. It was a sensation I hadn't felt in years.

I was used to the busy overwhelm of L.A. and almost forgot what it was like to just be still and process life fully and completely.

I knew starting over would not be easy, and it wasn't. Right away I went on a job search and, through a dear friend, was able to get hired almost immediately. I worked and pounded the pavement for nine months, never once receiving a penny from my son's father. I knew in that respect I was alone, but I couldn't be defeated, because my vision was greater than my circumstances. I knew that I wanted to spend time with my son, and that my end goal was to walk away from that job and have the freedom to be with him as often as possible.

The big day came. Labor started, and 36 hours later I became a mom to a beautiful baby boy! There is absolutely nothing in this life that will ever compare to holding a baby in your arms for the first time. There he was. I named him Asher, which means "blessing and happiness." After I chose the name, I realized that *he* was the reason! He was the purpose of me going to experience living in L.A. There is nothing else that could have made my life better in L.A. than walking away with this precious person who God gifted me with.

Through my surrender and prayerful life, I walked by faith, being constantly led in the right direction to bring a message of hope to those who had similar circumstances as me. Doors opened that I never thought possible, my personal business grew and expanded, and then went international. I later married and had three more little nuggets, which then made me a mom of four!

Experiencing the blessing of God's power in my life was powerful. I never stopped believing in the power of freedom and knew that the message I wanted to share was more powerful than anything I feared. Today, my life may not be perfect, but I still feel blessed beyond measure. I do all things out of love, and regardless of setbacks and challenges, I know that there is always a rainbow on the other side of the storm to see me through! We can always choose to create a new beginning!

Closer: Trailblazing Past Fear to Uplevel

Suzanne Duret

Suzanne Duret is a trailblazer. She has failed, succeeded, and everything in between. She has stared down fear, lack of knowledge, and powerful men, and stampeded through it all to discover innovative paths to success for herself and her clients.

Over the past 30 years, Suzanne has started eight companies, with no college education or formal training. Her very first business was a medical device company that sold for millions just 21 months after launching. She has success and expertise in growing careers and businesses, start-ups, innovation, and raising capital.

Suzanne is now committed to helping both professional and entrepreneurial women reach their next level. She coaches and guides with innovative and unique ways to achieve a goal, tackle an obstacle, or create an opportunity out of thin air. Suzanne offers numerous programs, including Painting the Vision and The Strategy Room. You can learn more about her by visiting SuzanneDuret.com

———

"What makes you think you can do *that*?"

I heard this from my mother a lot as a child—it was always her response when I said I wanted to do something *big*.

I was always coming up with new ideas, things I wanted to be or accomplish, and professions I wanted to try out: Become a movie director (still just a dream); go to electronics school (did it and was the only woman in the class); start my own business (I've started eight); write a book (done); live somewhere warm with water (Tampa Bay is now my forever home).

I realize now what a gift that was. Instead of letting my confidence and ambition be squashed like a cockroach, I believed I could accomplish anything I chose—and I was going to prove it.

So off I went. I skipped college to get out and experience the world.

My first leap was toward a game-changing career move after having worked as an administrative assistant. I lived in my home state of Minnesota at the time. My boss flew the receptionist and me to Florida as a thank you for our loyal work. We spent a week partying on his yacht with a staff of three waiting on us hand and foot. That first day was awesome!

The next day I decided I wanted to get the hell out of Minnesota and live in Florida. I spent the rest of the week visiting my boss's commercial real estate site he was building. I explored the project. Then I dug deep and uncovered that there were some underhanded activities going on.

Scared shitless, I pushed through my fear on that first day back in the office. I met with my boss and told him what I'd done in my spare time. I shared what I had uncovered, and offered proof. Then I told him he should hire me to manage everything for him at his Florida operation.

That was my "in," the first step to a job transfer that would lead to a pivotal career change.

I "painted the vision" that what I didn't know he could teach me, and reiterated that he already knew he could trust me. I drove home the initiative I took, the things I uncovered, and the drive I had to UPLEVEL. The next day, I received a huge promotion, a pay raise, and an all-expense paid relocation to Florida.

I moved one month later—and that was just the beginning.

Life is full of opportunities if you stay open to them, think creatively, and trailblaze past your fears lurking in the background. Every major career move in my life has been the result of creating a reality out of an opportunity and creating an opportunity out of thin air. We can all do this. I've proven it over and over myself and through the work I've done with my clients.

But I digress. After being transferred to Florida, my boss had to close the business within eight months. We discovered that his business partner was blowing all the Florida-based profits on cocaine. One thing led to another. Buh-bye awesome new job in Florida. Oh, I should mention that my marriage went bust during that time too. We had just bought a boat, got certified to scuba dive, and were digging into our new world.

But life throws curve balls. My marriage mess was another stressful layer that could have leveled me to the ground.

I picked myself up and decided to push past all of my fears and head-tripping to go for what I wanted in life. I turned down my boss's offer to take on a comparable job and move back to Minnesota, all expenses paid. Did I really want to leave beautiful Tampa Bay? Uh... *NO!*

Instead, I decided on a new career in a different industry, with a new life as a single person, and went after landing my next dream job. It wasn't easy. I had so many fears trying to take me down. That's when you either "lay or slay."

Guess what I did? I slayed, baby!

I created my next dream job out of thin air. Through that job, I met an emergency room doctor who had invented countless medical devices. He needed to raise capital and build a business around his inventions, but he was a busy doctor with a family and little time for all of that. So, we started talking and bounced some ideas around. This led to forming an agreement to start a medical company together. I had to go all in, so I walked away from my job. He worked more shifts in the emergency room to cover the overhead and to keep me afloat while I worked on raising capital.

That journey was one that movies are made of—one that brings entrepreneurs to their knees with suicidal thoughts and gives new meaning to being on a rollercoaster ride. No college education or formal training could possibly offer up the things I learned about business, people, and myself during this time.

One of my most notable and defining moments was when I was raising venture capital for this company. I sat across a boardroom table from three hardcore investors. These were older men not accustomed to seeing a "young cutie-pie" with no experience whatsoever trying to raise over a million in funding. (Keep in mind, this was the 90s.)

I sat quietly while they grilled my business partner. When they were done with him, they turned their sites on me. The lead investor pushed away from the table and sat back in his chair, legs spread, and arms crossed over his head as he smirked at me. The other two investors followed suit by pushing back their chairs and smirking at me.

Monkey see, monkey do.

"Well Miss Duret," said the lead investor, "It's obvious that you're only here because you must give great blowjobs." Before he had said a word, his body language already clued me in that he was about to try to annihilate me.

I wasn't caught off guard. I didn't cry, wince, scream, shrivel, run, melt down, or whatever it was they expected.

I calmly stood, closed my briefcase, and smiled as I reached across the table to shake the lead investor's hand as he remained sitting (this is power positioning). I said, "Well, Mr. So-And-So (name withheld), I came here to discuss business, not sex, and clearly, you're trying to f@&! with me."

I turned and left. As I waited at the elevator, I had no idea if my business partner would stay and throw me under the bus, or follow behind me. Nor did I care. I just learned something impactful about myself. By the time the elevator dinged, and the door began to open, my business partner came running; he had quickly packed up the product prototype and left the room.

The elevator ride down was quiet. As we walked out to the parking lot, he said he was proud of me. He said he wished I could have seen their faces as I walked out the door. Priceless. A few days later that lead investor called me and said he was impressed with how I handled things. He said he behaved the way he did to "test" me. Right! I told him there were better ways to test someone without being so rude and vulgar. I called him to the carpet on his B.S. and then told him I had no intention of "getting into bed with him," no pun intended.

A few months later, we closed on our funding of $1.2 million from professional venture capitalists who treated me with respect. They also appreciated that I passed their entrepreneurial tests with flying colors. I was made to jump through a few hoops and make some things happen before they made the investment.

Our medical device was tested in emergency rooms all around Tampa Bay. I spent back-to-back shifts in the ER when my business partner was on duty so that I could learn the medical lingo and witness the experience of nurses and doctors under extreme pressure. I saw crazy things that happened to people. I was deeply entrenched in the medical world here in Tampa Bay as we built that company. It was life-changing in so many ways.

21 months after my medical device company officially launched, it was sold for millions to a major medical company. I went on to start other businesses and write a book, *Inventing for Wealth*, which includes a foreword by Tony Robbins. The first time I met Tony was at a radio station in St. Petersburg where he was being interviewed prior to his big event in Tampa the next day. This was when I asked him to write my book foreword, and he invited me to appear as a success story in his television program.

My wish for any woman reading this story is that you BELIEVE you can achieve anything you set your mind to. Tampa Bay and our beautiful country are filled with opportunities all around us. Don't wait for those opportunities to magically appear; instead, you must get out there and make them happen!

About the Curator, Leigh M. Clark

Leigh M. Clark is on a mission to make an impact and live her legacy. From her busy career transforming businesses through technology, to her charity that throws around kindness like confetti, everything Clark works at is about making a difference.

Clark is an author with several Amazon bestsellers such as Living Kindly and The Dream is in Your Hands. She is embarking on a new series Slay the USA which features powerful women with purpose from cities across the United States.

Additionally, her nonprofit Kindleigh has made a significant impact nationwide in efforts such as painting and donating murals to other nonprofits, gathering school supplies for foster children, distributing crucial items to the homeless, delivering gifts to women and children who are victims of abuse and human trafficking, and paying off holiday layaways for strangers. Their work has been featured on Rachael Ray, The Today Show, and on many other national media outlets.

She is also a motivational speaker who has been featured nationally, including multiple times on the TEDx stage. Her hope is to inspire others to live their best life by sharing their own positivity. She believes that we can make the world a nicer place, one act of kindness at a time. Through helping to uplift others she has found her purpose and is leaving an indelible mark.